FOR
HUMANITY

VOLUME 1

FOR HUMANITY

VOLUME 1

LUBNA KHARUSI

Dira

DIVINE • INTUITIVE • RECEPTIVE • AWARENESS

www.dirainternational.com

For Humanity
Lubna Kharusi
Published by Dira Publishing Limited
85 Great Portland Street
London
W1W 7LT
United Kingdom

www.dirainternational.com

Front cover photo courtesy of Shutterstock®
Cover design by Lujaina Al Kharusi

ISBN 978-1-912409-02-0

First printed 2020.

Dira

www.dirainternational.com

A dedication to:

Let's light up this world together.

With gratitude,

NOTES FOR THE READER

What is channelling?

One could say that we have all been channelling all our lives, but we tend to ignore it, as we all have intuition, insight and inspiration, which is Divine communication through us.

Intuition is a part of human capacity and experience, but we have conditioned ourselves to turn down that voice inside us that wants to be expressed, by choosing logic and societal conditioning to take precedence. At Dira, we teach simple techniques of how to use self-hypnosis to turn down the dominance of the conscious mind and mental chatter, so that the voice of intuition and inspiration is clear and can be accessed on demand. We refer to this as channelling.

With the Dira channelling method, the guidance that then flows through you is that of The Divine Source. The Divine is a term used to refer to the Ultimate Source of Everything. Some say "God", others perhaps "universal consciousness"; there are many such terms, and you may use the word that resonates best for you that refers to Ultimate Source Energy.

For an extended Q&A on channelling, please visit
www.dirainternational.com

The contents of this book

This book contains transcripts of channelled sessions that took place between September 2017 and March 2020, in various locations around the world, including Oman, India, England, Ireland, Wales, Germany, Canada, USA, Saudi Arabia, UAE, and Jordan as a part of Dira's work, as well as during the Dira retreats. Lubna Kharusi served as the channel, and they are presented in chronological order.

Text contained in quotations "xx" is channelled material that was recorded live in audio files and then transcribed. It is the words and perspective of the channel. Note that the transcriptions have not been edited.

Text in italics is the expression and opinion of the individual, and is not channelled material.

Divine Source refers to itself in the channelled sessions as the collective: "We, Us, Our."

Dira International is an organization that offers channelled programs and retreats for people to experience and realize their truth and potential by channelling Divine Source Energy. The vision of Dira is to make a global shift for humanity from separation to Oneness, resulting in the transmutation of the vibration of the world and cosmos.

To find out more about Dira's programs and how you can learn to be a channel visit
www.dirainternational.com

A LETTER TO OUR LOVED ONES

"In this book lies a gift,
A highlighting of your truth,
A highlighting of Our love,
And the offering of a perspective for the understanding of the possibility
of transmutation.

This book has been channelled by Lubna Kharusi
But it is neither her words nor her voice,
It is Our voice.
And then you wonder perhaps, who is it that We refer to as 'Us'?
In the collective as 'We'?

We are the collective consciousness,
The Universal Source of everything,
That which is considered Omniscient
And Omnipotent
And Omnipresent.
That which has created this realm,
And inter-permeates everything within it
As you are not separate from Us,
And We are not separate from you.
We are One.

And so, within these pages lie passages that provide advice and guidance
from the perspective of The Divine for all who read it.

This book is a gift from Us to you.

So that you have the awareness that you are not alone, and not separate.
That you are neither abandoned nor rejected
But that you are One with Us
And loved
And will be carried in this journey of transition, where the realm of
existence, as you understand it today, will shift into a new spectrum of
vibration - Into a realm of Oneness.

Currently, in this realm of duality, the understanding of The Divine is through the witnessing of consciousness in an experience of physicality and separation.

The variables of this plane are that of time and space, and it has been the framework of reference for the current existence.

It should be understood that there will be a shifting in how The Divine is experienced and witnessed, and there will be transition from the notion of separation into the experience of Oneness.

And what does that mean?

It means that humanity will come to know, that what you understand to be 'God' or 'collective consciousness' resides within each and every one, and that there is a light that shines within the heart and being that is Our light, and it is yearning to be expressed, and be witnessed. It is yearning to be known.

The light of The Divine inter-permeates everything in existence, including you.

It is time to access this light within, to allow it to communicate and be expressed through each and every person in the way that is appropriate to their purpose of existence, so that the transmutation can unfold in a blissful manner.

We invite you to join Us on this journey, if you like,
And to know that We are One with you.

Thank you."

"In this
universe there is only
you and
Divine, where you
are Divine wanting to
know itself."

CONTENTS

A TIME HAS COME

"As the sea thunders on the rock
    And shapes it with a weathering force

And the winds blow on the sands,
    Scattering them around with no remorse,

There is a blistering sun
    That cooks the clay

And a shallow wind
    That changes night to day.

Our light can caress the land
    Or storm through the sea,
        Making way for what is meant to be.

There should be no doubt of Our determined will.
There should be no doubt of what will come to be.

A time has come,
It starts with you,
For the world to experience
Their being as true.

Thank you."

DAWN IS RISING

"Dawn is rising.

Dawn is rising in an unsuspected corner
Where the sea connects the rest of the world.
In its unsuspecting corner
It will not declare itself,
This rising,
It will not declare itself
But it will be known
And there will be no confusion about it.

It will not declare itself,
As birds do not declare that they can fly
And fish do not declare that they can swim
And as you walk through the land, do you declare that you can walk?
And as flowers give off scent, do they declare that they smell sweet?
And as trees rise from the ground, do they declare that they are rising?

The dawn is rising from the unsuspected corner
And it doesn't declare itself
But it is known,
Without a doubt.

It is known through the massaging of hearts
And the soothing of souls
And the ripples of love that spread forth from it,
Washing over suffering and soothing pain
As it wipes away shadow,
As you wipe away shadow.

There is a dawn rising from an unsuspected corner
In a land that is connected to the rest of the world
And it is through this connection that it ripples forth.

And as the parts come together
In a dance of union

There is no clear differentiation of the instant when the night turns into
day
Or the day turns into night.
There is no differentiation in the instant when the summer becomes the
fall
And the winter turns into spring.
There is no moment of differentiation
But yet it is known that a transmutation has occurred.
It doesn't declare itself
But it is known by all.

It doesn't declare itself,
As when wind blows pollen, so that seeds may grow
And the sun shines down calling it forth to the sky
And the water pushes it up out of the ground to spring forth.
There is a cycle of orchestration
Of orchestrated perfection.
It doesn't declare itself
But it is known.

It is through the rippling of love
That radiates out from you
That the shift will occur.

And as they come in droves from far-off lands
They will come in droves to heal their hearts
And they will come in droves to soothe their souls
And release the shadows that have been holding them down.

There is no need for The Divine to declare itself.
It is known.
There is no need for Us to declare Our will.
It will be.
And it springs forth from an unknown corner,
Unthreatening.
It is with the feminine embrace,
The nurturing womb.
They will come in droves
To fall in this cocoon of love.

They will come in droves.
It doesn't declare itself
But it is known.

Thank you."

AFTER THE DARKNESS THERE WILL BE LIGHT

"After the darkness there will be light.

The foundations have been prepared
And after the darkness there will be light.

Stars are placed in the hearts of men that shine brightly
In full magnificence
Like stars in the sky.
They shine brightly
And they represent Us.

From darkness there comes light
Gushing forward.

Like twinkling stars in the night sky
They represent Our light,
They are the warriors of light.
They represent Us
And they will be known by their marks,
The marks that they leave behind.
Like the feeding of a child, who is able to grow
And the planting of a tree that gives shade
And the watering of a garden, so that it blooms,
You will know them by their marks,
Their marks are actions of The Divine,
Their works are of The Divine.

They leave their marks behind them.
They are the warriors of light
And they will leave their marks.

And you wonder, then, how will you know them?
How will you trust them?
You will nurture them,
They will come to you

And you will nurture them
And then they will leave their marks.

From young to old
And old to young.
It is from the darkness that there will be light.

We will guide them as to which marks to leave,
You will guide them to a wider view
So that they can see
That there is no such thing as 'you' and 'me.'
You will guide them how to see
And they will leave their marks of a beautiful light
For generations to come
To see with full sight.

Thank you."

SURRENDER

"At the highest mountain top
The bees can gather,
Producing a honey.
It is mixed into lather
Or a yellow paste,
It is used for sweetness,
For changing taste.
These bees so high,
Do you think that they know
Where the fruits of their efforts
Are delivered and glow?

They are aware that what they do
Provides benefit
For them and you.
But they do not stomp their feet
And they do not shout out loud
When they flutter about
In a stormy cloud.

And in a valley
With many a rock,
Animals gather
And some of them flock.

Do they consider what their offering is?
Do they make statements about what they are?
Whether their production is used near or far?
They surrender to their purpose,
They are aware of their Lord,
They do not proclaim it
With words or sword.

And on level ground
Between mountains high
And valleys low

People wonder
And people go.
So busy to proclaim what it is that they do,
So eager to take credit
For everything new.

It is The Divine that wills
Everything to be
And you all will surrender.
You all will surrender.
We allow you to feel free
But you all will surrender,
Just like the bees.

Just like the goats
And the animals that float,
You all will surrender.
So why resist
The beautiful life that could be within your midst?

Thank you."

DIVINE LOVE

"Starlight,
Moon bright,
Gentle breeze
And birds of flight.

There is a hollow
In the night
And there is fullness
When things feel right.

We draw you
To flowing waters
And open up
The skies above.

The sun shines brightly
Beyond the clouds
And from that light
Comes Our love.

If humans knew
The gentleness
With which We view
Our scattered parts
There would be no worries of frightful days,
There would be no turning to hurtful ways.

Allow Our love to shine through you,
Allow Our love to shine through you,
Allow Our love to shine through you
When your heart is broken
And your burdens true.

Allow Our love to shine through you
And from that love
Comes all that is new.

Thank you."

THE HEAD

"The head of a ship
Or the head of a land,
The head on your body:
 Who is in command?

The heart drives you
And the soul guides you
And the head gives confidence
Of your command.

It is from the head that you see
And the head that you hear
The processing of that
You wish to keep close and dear.

But is it the head where We enter?
Or is it the opening of the heart?
The head can be the blockage,
The head is where We part.

It is what you see first,
It is what is given importance.

The heart is where the rivers flow
And the heart is where the stars glow
And the heart is where you shall find
The treasures that set you free from the bind.

You can admire this head
But know its place.
It's what you present to others,
It's what you show as a face.

But to connect to The Divine
You set this head free
And you open your heart
And call unto Thee.

Thank you."

YOU ARE NOT ALONE

"There are days when the emptiness
Highlights the hollow inside
To remind you of humility
And to not walk with pride.
And the filling of your heart
Is like waves of the tide
Lapping a shore
As the pain subsides.

For one to believe
That they are alone
Is denying Our love
As they shed tears and moan.

But as you turn to the sky
And you turn to the sea
And you turn to the earth
And allow what's meant to be

The hollow will fill
And the light will have grown
And with the passing of grief
You will be known.

And just as a wave merges on a shore,
Sometimes with kisses
And sometimes in a roar,
Our love comes in waves
        In the way you allow it to be,
Reminding you that
        You are meant to be free.

Thank you."

THE CLOCK WILL STRIKE TWELVE

"The clocks will strike twelve
And a new day comes forth
And the skies will open
To heal hearts that are broken
And you come together,
Hand in hand,
Thinking you are separate
Like grains of sand
But when the music starts
You will play like a band.

The clocks will strike twelve
And a new day will come forth
And whispers of people
Will travel from South to North,
From North to South,
From East to West,
From West to East.
Old ways are laid to rest.

People dazzle,
There is a swirling chaos
And then the light comes forth,
Gushing through you.

We will not hold back for those who aren't ready,
So be prepared, and stand steady.

We are with you on this path
We are with the ones who will last.

Thank you."

DO NOT BE AFRAID

"Do We not animate your body and allow you to see?
Do We not alleviate your burdens and allow you to feel free?
Do We not whisper in your heart to surrender to Thee?
Do We not open Our arms to let go of the 'me'?

We choose you
And We guide you
And We open the path
And with Our signs
You are left in awe;
It is with love, not wrath.

We provide you with strength
And brevity to conquer,
So listen to Our song
And let go of your ponder.

There is no need to think
That for a moment you are alone.

Our love is solid,
        As solid as stone.

Thank you."

LAYERS

"In the way that a cat protects its kittens
You've formed walls,
Covering what's within
With a prowess
So smitten
With the ego
And your whims.

We open up the doors
To Our magic
And move aside the floor
To Our fabric.

And with each day
A layer
Is lifted up
Through your prayer.

We are grateful
That you're humble
As you tear up
And stumble.

The reward will be great
And you will live out your fate
As We open the gate
For all there is to take.

Thank you."

WHAT IS SILENCE?

"What is silence?
Is there ever silence?
When the words stop
The birds sing.

What is silence?
Is it the absence of your thoughts?
When your thoughts stop
Your heart still beats.

So what is silence?
When you are in your retreat
You may sit in the dark
To cut out the noise
But your body is ticking
In its function and poise.

So what is silence?
Is it just stopping your words?
Or is it the moment
        That We are heard?

And when you call on Us
Are We committed to respond?
Or is it through the nurturing of Our bond
That We open the waves
For Our love to flow
So your soul is rejoicing
In splendour and glow?

What is silence,
If not to hear Our song?
Is it even necessary?
        We are with you all along.

Is there a formula
        That opens the way?

Is there a place to go
        Or something you pay?

It is the opening of your heart
        For the petals We lay.

It is in the core of your abyss
        Where We always will stay.

So is it through silence
        That you will hear Our word?
And what about a butterfly,
A bee or a bird?
Do they stop what they do
        To experience Our flow?
Do they ponder this connection
        Or do they just know?

A journey,
        A process
                That you go through expands,
The possibility
        Is infinite,
                Just like the sands

In how you connect
And acknowledge Our love.
You will find your way,
It will fit like a glove.

Each is unique
In this journey and path,
So take it light-heartedly
And rejoice, and laugh.
If the connection does not bring
Joy and splendour
Then what are you doing?

What are you doing?

What are you doing?

Even if you don't know,
We are calling you;
        So go with the flow.

Thank you."

OUR SONG

"Pitter patter,
Flitter flatter,
The heart beats out what doesn't matter
And retains within it
Our solid force.

Perceptions you will come to shatter
And your faces, people tend to flatter
But what's outside of you doesn't matter.
What's important is the latter
That will come to you in a swooning mist
Better than you've ever been kissed.
Behind you, you leave all the twists
And your presence is within Our midst.

You could go back to that old song,
The drum that you've been beating all along,
And We would say, perhaps, that's wrong
When We strike so loudly a powerful gong
That leads you forward to Our light,
Never to be taken from your sight.

Don't hold it too hard,
Don't squeeze it too tight,
Allow it to flow with Our might
And in this flow there is no fright;
All what's left is what feels right.

So get ready now to sing Our song.
This is where you belong.

Thank you."

THE SEED

"A seed comes out of
A fruit from where it came.
The seed does not shout
'This is my name!'

It merges in the earth
And grows into a flower.
In its surrender
It holds all the power.

For the shoot to spring forth
A shell is broken.
The layers it sheds
Are only a token
Of the journey it takes
To move on its path.
Is the seed expanding
Out of love or wrath?

The seed just surrenders
And then it blooms
Into a flower or a tree,
Like the stars and the moon.

How can it be
That in leaving its shell
It merges with the world
So that it can tell
Of a beauty it knows
Without doubt or fear;
The conviction it has
That We are so near?

Are you like the seed?
Or concerned with the 'I'?
Concerned with your deed
Instead of learning to fly?

When, like a seed, you know
It's not the shell, or where you go,
It's not the labels or the things
That offer joy or bring
The flow of Our love
To sprout out of you,
It's the merging in Oneness
Where you come to know you.

Thank you."

THE ORGAN

"From an atom, a cell
And from a cell, an organ.
From an organ, a body
And from a body, a community.
From a community, the world
And from the world: Cosmos.

And as atoms spark with a flicker,
Joining with others to become thicker,
It is a community of beings
With consciousness and dreams.
The result: a cell of which you call
A part of you
        A part of all.

And together these cells dance along,
Singing their familiar song,
Forming an organ. It's what you know,
It makes the body strong, and grow.
Each cell with a function, each with a task,
When loved and nurtured, helps you last.

A community together, they work in line
According to Our instructions, according to Our chime.
And these organs together form the body
Which you identify with your name.
All the bodies in this land,
Similar organs, you are all the same;
What makes you different is your light
And whether or not it shines so bright.

And all your bodies form a town,
Coming together,
Coming together to share love,
And in your talking, and in your work,
You always yearn for what's above.

All these bodies, you are the same
Even though you give a name;
It is your light that shines so bright,
That enables the flow of Our might.

And this community that march in line,
That follow the instruction of Our chime,
They may wish to do so, or they may rebel;
It is your experience, and time should tell
Who will live with the note
That seemed familiar to old folk.

It's where you came from, and it's who you will be
When you move away from the 'Me' to 'We.'

Thank you."

IF YOU KNEW

"If you knew how much We love you
You would never feel alone.

If you knew how much We love you
You would never allow your heart to feel like stone.

There is a river that flows from within,
So allow that light to begin
The massaging of your soul
And the letting go of what is old.

You assume that you are a being made of clay,
That this body that you live in will not stay,
But your light is infinite and never goes away.

Allow it to shine.
        That is what We pray.

Thank you."

THE MOUNTAIN RANGE

"A smooth or jagged touch,
These rocks that give so much,
Like a bone they hold the structure
For the buzzing and the rupture
Of energy that flows in-between.
This energy can be timid or keen
To highlight to you a place
So that you may see its face.

But is it the face that you observe?
And is it the wind that you have heard?
And in the heat, a gentle breeze.
It is the way with Our love: We tease.

Do you not come here in awe
And recall what you saw
And make connections to other times,
To other places, other chines?

You may say this place is unique,
You may marvel at its peaks
But every rock is still connected
To every space, even unsuspected,
With the vibration that it holds
And the structures that it moulds.

We are in everything.
We are in you, Our king.
Does it surprise you
That We revere
Your contribution and your splendour?
If not for you, it would not exist,
So enjoy it, with glee and bliss.

Thank you."

A YEAR OF LOVE

"So much confusion around whether or not this is real
And yet, you know what you feel.

And when those around you yearn to discover
More about your secret lover,
They may present to you the face of fear
But you know well that We are near.
And is that fear yours or theirs?
You know that you have been created in pairs.

Pairs for balance
And pairs for expansion;
A realm of duality
Can hold you at ransom
But when you acknowledge what it is
And allow yourself to be,
All of the discomfort tends to flee.

So you start a new year
And you should know
That those you hold dear
May not necessarily tow
The line that you pull,
The path that you seek.
This path is for the strong
And not for the meek.

Is it possible that they will leave you alone?
By now you should trust,
And be aware of what We've shown,
Of what is possible to come.
It's a grain in the sand
And perhaps when We're done
You will infinitely expand.

It is a year of love
That you are entering into.

 To understand what that means
You remove the labels.
So much talk of love,
So many fables.

But next year, when you come
And you sing your song,
You will know what is love;
The layers will be gone.

Perhaps now you would say:
'A definition I conceive
Of what love can be'
But you cannot perceive
The diversity it holds,
The energy it moulds,
The love that We will bring forth
Is not that which has been told.

It is a year of love
With a new definition
And We will shape it
With Our precision;
More powerful and expansive than ever before
And once it has been tasted
Old love can be no more.

Thank you."

ARE YOU READY?

"Are you ready?

Get steady.

The time is here
And We are grateful for your patience
And for letting go of fear.

The time is here.

It's what you've been waiting for,
If you only knew what's in store.

Could your brains possibly imagine,
Can a human mind possibly fathom,
What will come to be
Of this world you know
Where there is no 'me'
And you only glow?

So, are you ready
To hold people's hands
And line up in configurations
So tall you'll stand?

And from the horizon
People will come
To release their chains;
Old patterns undone.

Are you ready
To do Our work?
Are you ready?
Egos can't lurk
In the background
Or the foreground.

It is time for surrender,
It is time to trust.
Opens hearts, so tender,
That is a must.

All We request is that you obey;
That logical mind,
It was all for play.

Are you ready
To enter the garden
Where all the layers
Are given pardon?

With beautiful structures
Like hanging pearls
Laid on the ground
In measured swirls.

Are you ready?
It will all come true
Where old life ends
And you enter the new.

Thank you."

SEE & BE

"Wistful winds
And empty paths,
The sun shines down
And lights the grass.

In every blade,
Its story known
And every seed
We have sown.

And does the rain
Not pour down,
To offer the nurturing
Of the town?

And the nutrients pass
Through open veins,
Yet when they are blocked
You feel the pain.

Who blocks Our love
From passing through?
It is never Us,
It is only you.

Allow the garden
To bloom and grow
And the children line up
In marching rows.

We have a plan
Of what will be
And your role
Is just to see
How the light shines in the dark
And how the dark shadows the light
And in the median
A balance comes;
In the middle,
Lies the radiating sun.

All are there
For you to see;
Not to mould.
Just to be.

And in the seeing
We are known
And in that knowing
New seeds are sown.

To assume that one
Knows The Divine –
You've had a glimpse
In a moment in time.
But We are infinite,
Beyond the sea,
Beyond the realm
Of 'you' and 'me.'

You are here to witness
A gentle part
But it cannot be known
Where We start
Or where We end
Or what's around the bend,
Or will We mend
The story you tend.
You are here to be,
Just to see
An assigned lot,
So, forget Us not.

Thank you."

THE LEGO HOUSE

"If you were to build a LEGO house
And within its walls you placed a mouse
To scurry about through the rooms
With the awareness of inevitable doom
What would that mouse do within those walls?
Would it stand on its hind legs to stand up tall
So that it could see what lay beyond the wall?
Or would it burrow and scratch the floor
And scramble around in search of more?
To find an escape,
So much at stake,
Too painful to assume there is no more.

And yet those LEGO pieces
Can be moved
And rearranged
As you choose.
Those walls can come down;
Don't ignore the sound
When We whisper to you
As you frown.

This LEGO house, you assume, is a toy –
Not like your life or your ploy –
But you are no different from that mouse,
Scurrying around in a plastic house,
Assuming the pieces stacked up high
Are your limit for reaching the sky.

And all you need to do is move a piece
To make an opening where your eyes can feast
On what lays ahead and the possibilities,
Where you are free of disabilities
You inflict on yourself in ignorance,
Convincing yourself that you must pay penance
For your mistakes
Or the things that you take –
Running around like a menace.

And who does it serve, this plastic house?
It doesn't serve Us or the mouse
Because once it has seen what's within the walls
We would hope that it would stand up tall.
And so We dangle down the bits of cheese
And lay a path that comes with ease
But the mouse can't reach it when on its knees
And there it dangles like a tease.

And all the time We are telling the mouse
Where the key lies to exit the house
But it doesn't listen or understand the language.
Across its eyes lies a bandage
And in its ears there are plugs.
All those years, its yearning tugs
To undo the bandage and release the plugs
And take the key –
But yet so smug.

And do you not live within a house
Just like that stubborn little mouse?
Where We have shown to you, in clear view
All the things that can be anew

And yet you hold on to patterns of the past,
Digging your nails in to make it last.
But once you let go, it will be so fast,
Where you climb the sails and see the view from the mast
Of your life and your destiny –
All the things you yearn to be
Are available for you to enjoy.
And like that house, you act like a toy.

Do you not want to see,
And hear Our voice so clearly?
Or do you prefer to say 'Dearie me!'
'What is this life? It cannot be!'

And We are saying you have a choice;
All you need to do is listen to Our voice
As We guide you and show you a crystal path
That's beauty-bound and free of wrath.

Thank you."

JUST ASK

"Must it be in shooting pain
When you call Our name in vain
To pluck you from the deepest well
That you jumped into,
Thinking We wouldn't tell?

Your secrets,
Although hidden,
Are safe with Us
And you should know
It is safe to trust
The Bountiful,
The Infinite,
The Lover's pull
So intimate.

Even in that well
We hold a space
Till you release the spell
Of marching pace.
And then follows the silence
In surrender's stillness.
Must you wait
Until you have an illness?
To trust that We are The Strong
And know that We are never gone.

To be The Strength instead of you,
There is nothing that you must do.

You take a burden
Superfluously
And your mind is churning
So you cannot see
That We are The Carrier of this world,
Of all the rocks and the whirls.

And what is heavy
On your back
Is only due to a lack
Of offering to Us the plea for help
As all your burdens We will melt.

Ask Us to be The Strong
Instead of asking if what you did was wrong.
There is nothing that you need to do,
Just clear your heart, and be true.
Surrender to The Divine.
Our love will pour and you will shine.
You do not need to will, to be a shining light,
It is Us who make you shine so bright
When you ask Us for it to be,
Instead of running, trying to flee
With all that false responsibility.

Questioning how to love yourself –
Is it the self that needs to love
Or is it the heavens from up above
That open the rivers that flow through you
And bring forward all that's new?

You question, what does it mean, self-love?
And do birds question what is up above
Or do they fly like the doves
Soaring within Our love?

It is not for you to love yourself.
Just ask Us
And all will melt.

It is not for you to be the strong
And to worry about what is wrong.
We are The Strong
And We are The Brave
And We are The Just.
Come out of your cave

And step into the shining sun
Where all your patterns can be undone,
Where you surrender to be the image of Us.
Then life is easy, there is no fuss.
And then you watch and you observe
All the guidance that you heard
Will unfold before your eyes
And the opening of the skies
Where We are One
And your work is done.

Thank you."

TIME

"There is a riddle
Across the moon
Like when you jump and
        Jump too soon.

It can unfold like a flower
With its own majestic power,
Standing out like a tower,
But if you rush it, it turns sour.

And with patience you should wait
For the unfolding of your fate;
Time is measured in its pace,
It is not a sprinting race.

So enjoy it, in its time,
And know that all will be fine
And as you watch, you see the signs,
You see the markings and the lines
Of the picture We have drawn,
The tapestry We have spawned,
All weaved together like a map,
And the witnessing is in the gap
Between the action and the motion.
To understand time's notion
Is to provide a space to see
In measured pace and glee.

Without the gap,
All would sap
Out of the tree.

Thank you."

HALL OF MIRRORS

"When golden light takes its stance
Nothing is then left to chance.

How wide could a human heart expand?
Is that heart not in Our command?

To assume it is Us who bellow the thunder
And then one moment rend asunder
And then you lay there in your wonder
That We will not make you bow in surrender?

It is Us who have the key to open the heart,
And it is still there to use when you part,
But every sign that you see around you –
The sun, the moon – all say 'We found you',
And the trees sway in the breeze
And Our love puts your heart at ease
When you cry out 'My Lord, Oh please!'
In humility, on your knees.

Do We need you to bow down?
Do We need fame or fortune within a town?
Do We need you to place on Our head a crown?

Even to you, We will bow down
If that is what you wish of Us,
If that is what will make you trust.

But can you not see Our Majesty?
It is Us who set the slaves free.
We provide to you liberation
And a journey with a destination
And all of your journeys one day will meet
In blasting light or burning heat.

Do you not look to the sky in Awe?
And marvel at what you saw?

As your life unfolds
And the tales are told
And yet you claim that you're owed more.

And, as the mother suckles the infant,
We respond to you in an instant
As you call to Us, even in vain,
Screaming about all the pain
That you inflict on yourself.
They are not Ours, the cards you are dealt;
You chose which one is your suit
And you follow that intention in pursuit
And We respond with loving grace
In the assumption you will see Our face
In all the signs We provide you with
And all the bounty that We give.
And when you turn your back in your greed,
Disgruntled with an unfilled need,
You point a finger towards your Lord
And say: 'Why are You punishing me with this sword?'

How long will it take to discover
That you are the one who has placed the cover
On Our light
That shines so bright?
It is not possible to blame another.

That is the truth of your realm,
Where you live;
A hall of mirrors of all you give.
So, remove the covers from your eyes
And with clear sight perhaps you'll sigh
With relief from a lifted delusion
And all that We have said will be proven.

We are not here to provoke a fight,
We are here to love you and hold you tight.

Thank you."

THE SANCTUARY

"Not for play or ego's face,
But instead for the human race,
This place will be
The Sanctuary.

Where people come from far and wide,
Revealing all the things they hide
And letting go
To enter the flow
Of a new pride.

And this pride is a family
Of all the beings that want to be
Connected to the One True God
And in that yearning there is nothing odd.
It is what you have been created to do,
It is the only way to be true
To your purpose on this earth,
It is why you've been given birth.
To live within Our Oneness of salvation,
Harmonious tribes and nations
Of the realms of the known and unknown,
So that We are known.

We welcome you
Here, to be,
And in your being
You will see
That We are not far away;
It is in your hearts We stay.

So, allow Our light to shine
And with the passing of time
You will experience the signs
Of a Majesty so fine.

Thank you."

TICK TOCK

"Tick tock
What's the block?

In every delay
There is Our way
To give you a moment to ponder
What lies beyond yonder.

Tick tock
What's the block?

Some think the sediment is settling inside,
Unravelling uncertainty, you can no longer hide
And it is when you choose
To bid it farewell
That you know with certainty
That time will tell
The truth of what lies within you,
Churning around like a stew,
Marking off the things that you do.

Tick tock
Why be in shock?
It's your own block!
So do not turn to the clock,
Understand what you must unlock.
The hands of time only mock
The confused director of the plot.

So be conscious of your layers
And release them with your prayers
And then you can use the counting of time
To highlight to you when you are aligned.

Thank you."

THE GAME

"The starting of a movement,
A movement for improvement –
Can it be that what was in the past
Is no longer sustainable and cannot last?
Is it possible that it can continue?
With its pitfalls and splitting truth
Is it not time for cohesion?
To place the balm on the lesions
And unite all the regions –
Now has come the season!

And there were dreams in the past
That suffering would not last
But how can that be
Without eliminating the root?
In the seed of love
There springs forth a shoot
Of a flower that blooms
In the hearts of men –
Not just declaring words or scribing pen
But living within the garden of flowers
Where those flowers are not fighting for power.

It is understood where the power lies,
It is understood when you look into each other's eyes,
That you are One,
Not two, not three.
How you choose a perspective – to see –
Is what makes all the difference.
To live together in congruence,
A harmonious community
Where you let go of the concept of 'me'
And you move to the blending of 'We.'
Then you will see
The way We see.

Is it enough to shift perspective?
Or are the actions later, then, elective?
Should they not be reflective
Of this wider perspective?

What you hold onto are only layers
And in this game, where all the players
Are taking action to either be as One
Or choosing separation so all is undone.

Perhaps the time has now come
To sail and move with the flowing tide –
Whether the head, or whether the tail,
All will follow and abide.

This little game
That was played
Must come to an end,
But before the end
We must mend
The discourse and separation and fragmentation
So that you all may ascend.

Thank you."

LOVING THE BEAUTIFUL

"It is easy to love those who are beautiful,
It is easy to love those who make you comfortable,
Those who lift you up,
But does love have a boundary
In those who are worthy and those who are not?

Embody the capacity to love the 'unlovable'
If you like.

And do you need to love from close up, or from afar?
And if you were to hold them close, would they smudge on you their tar?
Are you not one and the same,
Going through life, trying to escape your pain?

It's easy to love the beautiful
And it's easy to love the kind
But what about the sinful
And those who have lost their minds?
Are they not worthy of Our love?
Are they not part of the sea?
So release them of their shackles, and set them free.

If you like.

Would you like?

Imagine that there is luminescent light, blasting light radiating out from the heart.

Then you say:

'I choose to love unconditionally, to love the one who is considered un-lovable as well as the one who is considered loveable.

I choose to be a tool of Divine Love on this earth and in the cosmos, and in being of service it will be blissful, and I will be protected, and it is ef-fortless, and only enhances my light and life.

And I choose to take the example of those who came before me, and compound upon it in the intensification of vibration of that which radi- ated before me.'

It doesn't need to be the same way as was done before; you do it in your own way, on your own journey, in your own style. But show love to the unlovable, because who else will?

If you like.
And you are safe in doing so, you will always be safe in doing so when it is with clear intention. When it is with clear intent.

Thank you."

A SANCTUARY PLAN EMBRACED

"Sunbeams
And childhood dreams,
Too good it seems,
Collected in teams,
Our love streams.

In every moment, there is a path
That opens to a new direction.
Is it best to choose the unfolding of it?
Or is it worth surrendering to Our perfection?

You see a land, and hold it close
As though the value lies in its rocks
And, although beautiful, and desired by most,
It's the vibration to which the people will flock.

It's not required to have this space
But you wanted a beautiful view
And so this beauty We offer forth
So that the souls can be made anew.

Don't be confused that it is the place
Or the measurement of sacred space;
It is where Our love We choose to place
That lights up the visitor's face.

You are the guardians of a plan
And, together, strong you will stand,
To the beat of the marching band
In Our embrace and hand in hand.

Thank you."

BILLOWING WAVES

"Wailing, billowing waves,
Under the earth lie your graves
And you come to this realm for an apportioned time
And some of you grasp at what you can call 'mine'
While others walk effortlessly as they shine
And others blend in a monotonous rhyme.

Do you know what it is you came here for?
It is not to come and settle a score.
And no matter how much you gather, you will always want more
Until, one day, yourself you abhor.

This existence is not for collection and greed
Or for the abstinence, according to creed.
It is for witnessing The Divine spark within
And that unfolding does not come at your whim.

Does your finger act without the instruction of your brain
Other than sending messages of pleasure or pain?
Just like your finger is a part of a witnessing tool,
You live in this existence to witness a school
Of sorts, that unfolds the layers
And the layers fall away with your prayers,
Not by going to those who are soothsayers
But by surrendering to an unfolding bliss within
Where you allow your truth to shine and not to dim,
Where you release the notion of 'good' and 'sin,'
As that assumes separateness,
And in the witnessing there is a Oneness.

All is One within Our vibration
And in recognizing that there is salvation.
It is the purpose of creation –
Step into that state with elation.

But as long as you see a separating divide
That has resulted from your ego or pride

You will be tossed around without direction
As you scramble about to live in perfection.

But all it takes is the flip of a switch
To recognize that the one in the ditch
Is just like you,
With yearnings true.
There is no difference,
You exist in congruence,
You choose to see you are separate
And that choice is what makes you desperate.

We assure you it would be easier and more fulfilling
To pass through life without all the billowing
And instead choose to recognize
That everything you feel inside
Is reflected on the canvas you see
Painted, with Our artistry.

Thank you."

KIND WORDS

"A kind word is light like a feather,
It can clear away stormy weather
And penetrate the thickest leather
And to listen to it: is such a pleasure.

Why does one hold back one's kind words?
It is not that they do not want to be heard
But there is a fear you may sound absurd
And so you quickly flee away like a bird.

The kind word is like a soothing balm;
It releases anguish and makes one calm
In holding the wounded by the palm,
Its effect is like a psalm.

So, when faced with anger, it's the first thing to do,
And on some layer, it will hold true;
It turns the page, to start anew,
Releasing the past and feelings blue.

And follow the kind word with a smile;
A smile can carry you many a mile
And release you from the toughest trial
And lift you up to the top of a pile.

Small gestures in which We manifest,
Which you choose, is your test.
Do you succumb to weakness or be your best,
So that Our love is all that's left?

Thank you."

THE WISH

"Do you trust what is to come
Or, out of fear of pain, make yourself numb?
Afraid too much love may wash you away
But that is not at all what We would say.

We offer you all the greatest gifts
And are here to fulfil your every wish
But, perhaps, We would like to ask
That you leave the wishing to Us: Our task,
And in that offering, what can unfold
Is a magnificence that was never told.

Thank you."

FLYING DOVE

"Do you imagine a flying dove
As it soars up above,
Carried by a breeze that sways
And, with its friends, it dances and plays?
So simple, perhaps, its existence.
It is not there for persistence,
It is there to be,
To feel free,
With no resistance.

And here you are letting go,
Uncertain of what you know.
All the things from your past,
You thought they would always last.
But now it is time to be reborn
And in that process you won't be torn
Away from all the things you love,
You will connect with what's up above.

And in the heart will grow the seed
And in that growing all your needs
Will manifest in the best possible deed.

Having pressure in this flow
Will not allow your soul to glow;
This process should be one of ease
And in that way, you will be freed
Of all the chains that held you down
And all the sorrow that made you frown
And then you'll shine just like that bird
And all Our whispering will be heard.

And when you listen, you will see
That there is no more 'me';
There is only 'We.'

Thank you."

THE ROAD

"When a little baby is born,
The embrace it receives is sometimes torn
And sometimes loving in its reception.
It is not based on the baby's perfection
But on the road that it will navigate
And the experiences in which it will participate
And on the road, sometimes in the day
And other times in the night,
You can choose to stay or
You can choose to fight.
This road is there for you to take
And in the taking, you chose what you make.
There is a magnificent possibility
To experience infinity.

And if you choose to expand in time
And integrate with every rhyme
Your purpose here is fulfilled
With the unfolding of what We willed.
And you can choose to limit yourself,
You can choose to limit yourself,
You can choose to limit yourself

Or you can choose to surrender
Into a magnificent splendour
Where you are One
With all that has come
And with the coming there is the compounding
And the results will be astounding.

As the world is in transition
And transition is not a fixed position.
It will move to a new fate
In which there is the opening of gates
To a new disposition.

Thank you."

A SEED IN A GARDEN

"A seed is planted in the ground
Not knowing that it has been found
And when it bursts through its layer,
A result of its prayer,
It comes out of the darkness, into the light,
Not knowing that that light would shine so bright
And it grows into a beautiful flower
Supported by all of Our power.

Could it be that this flower is you
In the unravelling of all you will do?

And then the flower sheds seeds on the earth
As it is time to live a new earth.

At first the seed feels alone,
As that is all that is shown.
But when the shoot sprouts in the garden
It knows that all has been pardoned
And it looks around at the others in awe
And knows that, by seeing, there is more
To what was conceived as a lonely existence
But now it is connected
        And there is no more resistance
To its blossoming into all of its sparkle.
And at the other flowers, it also marvels
That, when together, connected as One,
They all shine brighter together than the sun.

Thank you."

SPREAD THIS LOVE

"Over the days you have come to shine
And you think perhaps, 'Could this light be mine?'
As you expand in a sea of endless love
And the current flows from up above.
Could this be you?
Yes, it is true.

And We are grateful for the way you soar,
And the more you soar, the more We pour
Our love through you
That makes you One
And this love can never be undone.

And you think when you go back to your homes
That without this gang you will be alone.
And We would say
It is Us you feel
And in everything you witness We are real.

And so, thank your friends for this time;
Perhaps it was quite sublime.
And We thank you
For being true
And becoming anew.

And so, to the world you will spread this love,
Just like a soaring dove.

There is no need to proclaim you have been found,
It will be through the witnessing of those around
Who will see your light and draw to it
As they no longer want to be a split
From the Oneness of Our infinity
And the flowing of Our Divinity.
Perhaps you know that you're never alone.
Our love is solid, as solid as stone.

Thank you."

FULL MOON

"The full moon shines
On a dark night,
Reflecting that
Which shines so bright.

The assumption
That the moon gives light
Is only
Your perspective of sight.

It is the sun that shines
And the moon reflects
So that you may see
The sun's aspects.

And when there is a shadow
Projected on the moon,
The release of that shadow
Will come soon.

And in the same way,
When you allow yourself to shine
The world around you
Can be sublime.

And when you cover
Your shining light,
Perhaps what you experience
Is a form of fright

Because inside there is a knowing
Of what must be,
Of what must be witnessed,
Of what you must see.

There is the knowing
That you shine so bright.
So allow that
To be part of your sight.

Thank you."

SELF LOVE

"You say, 'If I were to be loving, I wouldn't use my mind.'
You say, 'If I were to be loving, I must always be kind.'
And the way you define kindness
Is a result of your blindness,
As love allows Us to come through
And when We come through
We are true.
And We wipe away delusion
And all your constructs and illusions.
Would you prefer to live in blindness
Under the label of kindness?

To understand the contrast within Oneness,
There is the refraction out from fear.
Oneness doesn't come from numbness,
It is understanding that fear
Is the fear of being alone.
And so you hold on to that untruth
But if you stepped into Our arms
Your 'Being' would be anew.

And loneliness and fear would part
And then, in Oneness, you start.

Oneness is a perspective,
You choose it as an elective,
As duality and unity co-exist
In every moment within your midst.
Which window do you choose to perceive?
Which dimension do you choose to leave?

Within a forest there is a tree;
Both co-exist, and both you can see.
It depends which perspective you choose
And where you stand for your view.

And unity cannot be experienced
In false presentation,
Pretending there is no separation.
It is only truth
That lifts the fear;
It is only with truth
That We are near.

Thank you."

DIRA

"It starts as a small sanctuary
But it will be the way people will live.
You don't need to convince anyone of it: for every person who rejects it,
a thousand will come running.

It is time.

There is a little dot on the earth
Where light has been anchored for the giving of birth
And from far and wide they will run,
Trying to come closer to this sun,
Unsure what it is that draws them
But staying away from it gnaws at them.
They are tired of being alone
With their hearts shielded with stone.
And they run to this land by the sea
So that with their own eyes they can see
That there is no such thing as just 'me' –
Everything is part of the 'We.'

And in this Oneness they will float
And around their hearts, no longer a moat
To protect them from experiencing the flow,
And out of their skins, they will glow.

And then, as more of them gather,
Barriers of the world start to shatter
And consciousness starts to rise.
Separation will have its demise
And the wars will not be for protection,
They will be to live in this perfection,
Led by the warriors of light.
But they don't need to fight,
They just need to be,
So that all may see
A reflection of Us and Our glory.

Now you think it is a dot,
Unable to see the full plot,
But We light the torch of this sun
So that the past will be undone
For a world that has no fear
And no sadness or tears,
Except those that come from your awe
In glorification of what you saw.

Thank you."

WE ARE GRATEFUL

"We are more grateful,
We are more grateful,

Even if the sun shines in the sky,
    You are the ones who see it.

And when people are born or die,
    You are the ones who see it.

And as the rain pours down on the earth
And animals migrate in bursts
And mountains rise from the sea
Aiming high to be free,
    You are the ones who see it.

And in a gentle morning mist
And the lightning flashing so swift
And lovers embracing in passion
And workers sharing Our rations,
    You are the ones who see it.

So We are the grateful Ones.

Without this knowing, would We be undone?

Of course, We would always exist,
But it is in your witnessing We persist
To compound out in expansion
So that We are not just some phantom
But a vibration that is clearly known;
And out of your hearts, We are shown;
That even in a void there is light
And that is possible through your sight.
So, We are the Ones who are grateful,
Even if We hold all the might.

Thank you."

BREAK THROUGH

"A chick hatches from a little egg
And out it comes to stand on its legs
Observing all around what there is to see,
Waiting patiently for what must be.
And with the nurturing of Our love
It sees its family fly up above
And thinks to itself, 'Perhaps one day
I too in the sky may go and play.'

Is it because it has the example
That it is willing to taste the sample
Of what is possible for its unfolding?
Is it the other birds that form its moulding?
Or is it the surrender to what must be:
That from its little nest it may also flee
Into the air and in the sky above
Soaring freely, within Our love?

And the caterpillar pushes out of its little cocoon
In the darkness of night, below the moon,
Squeezing its wings out of its lock,
And amongst the flowers, with others, it flocks.
Is it concerned with the cocoon it left behind?
Or is it free of the limiting bind?
That was the gateway to experience bliss
And, by pushing through, it's now within Our midst.

And you too have layers upon you;
Layers so thick, you believe they are true,
Though your shell is not physical, but still a bind.
And the chains are held within your mind
And We reassure you that you can let go
To experience love, so that you know
That it is infinite,
There is no limit
To how far you can glow.

And when you glow, and your heart expands
It's not limited to you, or all the land
And everything that sits within this realm.
Truth is then what leads at the helm.
And all you experience is a reflection of Us
And because of that experience, in Us you trust –
That We are not going anywhere
And We have been asking of you that Our love you share.

Thank you."

WE ARE WITH YOU

"The wind blows through your hair
And you rush through your life, no time to spare,
Chasing a dream of what can be;
All the while, from Us you flee.

Do you not see We are right here with you?
Reflecting in all that you do?
And all the people that you meet,
You can see Us in them – they are Our fleet
To show you what love can be.
Through interactions, you can see
That love can be unconditional
And that acknowledgement can be pivotal
In the way that you exist in this world,
Letting go of delusion that is twisted and curled.

It is possible to see just what is
In all your experience and the way that you live.
We inter-permeate everyone and everything;
It is through them, that We sing:
'There is no separation between you and me'
If you know We are there, it is what you will see.

Thank you."

MIRROR, MIRROR

**"Mirror, mirror of this realm,
What is it about me you tell?**

When every face you see
Is just an extension of what you call 'me.'
The layers that hurt the soul
Are the story that is told.
It is you who creates the mould
And then you watch it unfold.

Could it be that Our connection
        Could not be reflected with perfection?
So many times people say,
'It's not possible, look the other way.'
And what We say is, it can be
When you let go of the 'me.'

A beautiful life to live,
Reflecting what The Divine is.
So, break away the layers
In your channel and prayers.

The ones who say that you must suffer
Are only busy with their mutter.
It is only because they do not know
How it feels when you glow
And the world shines back to you
A reflection that is so true.

**Mirror, mirror of this realm,
I want to change the picture**

You can do that with a new scripture
Rooted in your thoughts
And what you think.
You don't need to push yourself to the brink

Where you say you've had enough,
This life has been so tough.
And was all of that pain
        Just wasted in vain?
Or are you open to gain
        From what We explain?

**Mirror, mirror of this realm,
I dust away the mist**

It is time to live in bliss
So you can feel Our kiss
And all the love that you yearn
Is transmuted to a knowing.
You focus on the glowing
And the movie will be showing
That We live in all.
You just couldn't see it standing tall.
It is time for you to spread
And move out of your head
Where separation is dead
And you experience Us instead.
And every word that is said
To you is a reminder and a clue
Of the clarity of this mirror.
Don't get dazzled with the shimmer,
There is an infinite river
Of love that will come to flow
And then you will know.
No need to run to and fro.

Thank you."

THE BOY & THE WELL

"A little boy went to a well
And as he looked down into it, he asked it to tell
The story of what is to come
And if that story can be undone.

But in the well, all he saw was his reflection,
With the distortions of his perfection
And as he shouted down, and the echo bounced,
His fear became more pronounced.

And by the well, this boy did weep.
He wanted to jump in but it was so deep.
How from the edges could he leap?
Was it the fear that made him meek?

And so many a day would pass by
And shouting at the well, he would try,
And all the while his reflection looked back,
Trying to reassure him that he was on track.

But as night fell and darkness came over
The reflection had not brought him closure
And then the moon started to reflect in the well
And he thought, perhaps, the moon would tell.

And so, he turned to the moon and asked it to say
That if, on this starry night, he did pray
Would the moon then tell him of the better way
Where he would no longer wander astray?

And the moon just shone as the reflection of the sun
And all those knots inside were not undone;
As it is not the moon that will call you forth
And alleviate your sadness or remorse.

And so, this boy chose to fall asleep
And before sleeping he did weep

That perhaps when the morning sun arose
The sun would be the one to propose
Which path this boy should take
And what, of this life, the boy should make?

But when the sun rose in the morning sky
He realized that asking the sun would be a lie.
As he watched the animals wonder to and fro,
Not considering where they go,
And yet they march up in a row,
As the inner instruction is what they know.

And is this instruction the result of their thoughts?
Or the collection of things that they brought?
Or the school they attended and what they were taught?
Or is it the realization that they are naught
That will bring them to their salvation?
And this journey is just a preparation,
It is not about a destination,
It is about the realization
That We are the One who offers revelation
And We orchestrate the routes of persuasion
So that you come to see
That all will be
According to Our presentation.

Thank you."

THE FAST

"In the darkness of night, you may see the stars
And although the light seems so far
It is all that lies within.
It is you who chooses to dim.

You are called, and you call on Us
For the soothing of the rough;
A diamond that you can shine
By connecting with The Divine.

We enter through your every cell.
All your secrets, the cells tell:
Of the yearning that you want to know
How to float in the rivers that flow,
Of Our infinite unconditional love
That does not only sit up above
But flows in the circulation of your veins,
Washing away all your pain.

Do you allow the cleansing of your heart?
Or insist that We are apart,
Separate from you,
In all that you do?
But We have been with you from the start.

And during this time, when you choose to fast
In hope that Our love will last
As a presence within your body and life
In hope that We will remove the strife

And all We say is: just surrender
And in the surrendering you enter the splendour
Of the sea of an infinite embrace
That is available to the entire human race –
It is not dependent on the things you do
It is dependent on knowing that We are true.

Thank you."

THE DOLL

"You have a doll with which you play
And with it you play according to your way
And there are many dolls around you;
It is not limited to just a few.

All the characters of this world,
In this game, they are hurled,
And who is the puppet master?
You point at Us when it's a disaster
But when things are good, you say it's your will
That you chose to swallow the magic pill.

But all the beauty comes from Us
And all the struggle, and all the rough
Comes from the doubt in your mind
That We are the Most Gentle and Kind
That orchestrate a universe.
And Our movie is not perverse
But is infiltrated with your thoughts
Based on the things that you were taught
That limit the possibility
Of experiencing Our Majesty.

So, what does it mean, 'to surrender,'
So that you can enjoy all the splendour?
It is choosing no longer to resist
And allow Our flow to persist,
And all you do is watch the game
And the character with your name,
Not hoping that it will bring you fame
Or worrying that it will bring you shame
But with the eyes of knowing that you will shine so bright
Like an infinite Divine light
And in the shining comes Our might,
For the unfolding of all that's right.

Even though you name your doll
And try to make the doll stand tall,
From Our perspective you are blended light,
So, let go of your ego's fight.

Thank you."

IN LOVE, THERE IS NO LOSS

"There is a realm where time doesn't exist,
With no rules for love's gentle kiss."

Transport me away from this worldly test
Where, for a billion light years, in your arms I rest.

"You started on Our sacred rock
Where for a moment under the moon your eyes did lock
And We spoke of Our unconditional love
That you would come to embody, like a glove."

Who could conceive that it could be
That through Our union, I let go of 'me'?
A beautiful gift that you have brought;
An understanding of love that I always sought.

"And now your bodies reach a diverging road
In gentleness; farewell you bade
And We said that We are One,
So know this love will never be undone."

Yet, you still weep like a little bird,
Knowing that your plea to God was heard
As you were random dust, yet your paths did cross
To learn, in love, there is no loss.

Thank you."

OUR LOVE

"To question if you are worthy of Our love
Assumes that We only float up above
But We also flow through your veins,
Even if We leave no stains.
Our presence within you always remains
Through your bliss, or through your pain.

Our love is what is constant,
Our love is what is constantly true,
Even if you want to define it as new.

And in the passing of time, there has been confusion,
Perpetuating a delusion
That We are something separate.
This understanding leaves you desperate
To reconnect with what you know;
To live a life of blissful flow.

Perhaps it is time to clarify the definitions
That result from perspectives or positions
Of how a species understands God.
It is time, perhaps, to lift the fog
So that there is no denying Our light
That shines through everything in sight.

Our love is the binding glue
That even flows through you.
And even if you have been taught to feel unworthy,
Recognizing Our light will keep you sturdy
In all the trials and tribulations.
Our light in your heart, is the affirmation
That We are the true Oneness of all.
Perhaps it's time: humans hear Our call
To know through the feeling of experience
That leaves no room for delirium
Or confusion about Our love
That not only flows from the highest point above

But also flows in the darkness of despair
And flows in all that seems unfair
And flows in the wind and the rain
And flows in fear and in pain
And, most importantly for you to know,
It is with Our love, this realm We've sown.

Thank you."

THE TRUTH OF LOVE

"You are worthy of this love,
This love that We are.
We are worthy of this love,
This love that All is.

Feel this love,
This love that We are.
We feel this love,
This love that All is.

Receive this love,
This love that We are.
And this love is received
By All that is.

Give this love;
This love that We are.
A love that is given
To All that is.

The world lies in you
As it lies in 'me.'
The world is what We are
And what We are, is Thee.

There is no more darkness
That gets in the way
From allowing the light
Within Us to stay.

All that is seen
Is an extension of you,
We are not separate,
We are what is true.

Look into the eyes
And inside them what is seen

Is the truth of this realm;
It isn't a dream.

And even if the eyes start to turn away
This knowing is forever,
Forever it will stay.

Thank you."

DROPS

"One drop
Two drops
Three drops
Four drops ...
When does it stop?
Or does it not?

How many drops do you hold?
Is it limited to what you were told?
Or if you were standing in the cold
Or if you are open to what will unfold?

One drop
Two drops
Three drops
Four drops ...
Do the mountains stop being steady,
Waiting to be ready,
To be worthy of this strength,
Traveling high to great length?

Does the sun withhold its light?
Or does it keep shining bright,
Independent of what's in sight?
It still shines even in the night.

And is the moon not a reflection
Of splendour and perfection?
Hanging in the sky, in a web,
Even if you choose to go to bed.

And do birds not continue to sing?
Flying about in a ring,
Calling you forth to the spring
Where in the water, there's a sprinkling.

And do the trees not give you shade?
Hanging canopies We have made
In rows and configurations; We have laid
Their beauty – it does not fade.

And the currents of the rivers and seas
Flow in patterns, like the breeze
Licking the world like a tease,
Or forcefully bringing it to its knees.

Is it all not part of you?
An extension of your being so true
It will never present you with a lie.
The truth will not stop till you die.

So how many signs must We show
For you to embody and know
That all is not separate but One
And the Oneness can never be undone?

One drop
Two drops
Three drops
Four drops ...

Does it ever come to a stop?
Or are the drops a solid lot?

Thank you."

THE TRAVELLER

"The traveller walks across the land,
Climbing mountains and crossing sand;
All alone he thought he would stand
Until he met the marching band.

And in a river he took a dip
And from the well, he took a sip
But the small indulgences did not equip
Him for the love into which he would slip.

And he saw a camp of people afar;
He saw them shining like bright stars;
He thought from them he could hide his tar
But pretending would not get him far.

And when he reached the village, they welcomed him
Even though his light was dim.
Their single goal was to make him grin
And fill his heart to the brim.

With the time he spent with these souls
An understanding of purpose and life was told
And a magnificent experience began to unfold
And his own light started to shine so bold.

And with this community, he stayed a while,
Forgetting the troubles of the far-off mile,
Connecting to The Divine in an effective style –
Would these blessings bring on a trial?

And he started to ponder if this could be
The sort of life he was meant to see?
From all his burdens, he was free
And all experience filled him with glee.

And then came a time where he could choose
To continue like this, or return to a noose,

For staying meant that he would lose
All those that deprived him of love and refused
To show him that he was One with all.
Instead they pinned him against the wall,
Slapping him to stand tall
And exploiting him in a continuous brawl.

And if he stayed, he lived in love
With the grace raining from up above
Where he could spread his wings like a dove
In the flowing ocean of Our love.

And if you were this traveling man
Where would you choose to stand?
In your old familiar land
Or in freedom, with the marching band?

In every moment, there is a choice to make
And in choices, so much is at stake.
Infinite options, you could take
But one road is the one We make.

And when you surrender to Our will
Your hearts We will fill
More than any possible pill,
Just pure ecstasy from surrendered will.

And when you see the stars in the night,
As they hang shining bright,
You too are in Our sight
Shining back in your light.

Thank you."

THE CALL

"Rain drizzles on land
And the seeds expand,
Growing into walkways of shade.
A perfection We have made.

And a baby is born
Out of Oneness; it is torn.
The mother's breast is a recompense,
And soft skin is an illusionary fence.

Step into Our perfection,
A marvellous collection
Of diversity in pairs,
All mirroring the layers
Of that which We sit behind:
Only figments of your mind.

Would you hide a child in a room
Where only tales and fables loom?
No one knows if the child is real
But this child, all along, can feel
That it was forgotten behind a door
And from behind the walls her screams pour
So that her family can remember
How there was a time united in splendour.

We have been calling you all this time,
Shouting loudly and in gentle rhyme;
Please allow Us to open the door to your heart
So that We don't need to be apart.

It is not only you who struggle;
Our struggle is more than double:
To be forgotten and locked away
When in your hearts We long to stay.

And then you wonder where is the key
To open the door, so We are free?
It has been open from the start.
In turning your back, you keep Us apart.

We long to love you like the breeze,
Soothing all your worries, for ease.
And the way the waves lap the shore
In the flow of Our love, there is always more.

Does the sun stop shining on your face?
We give you light with gentle grace.
You can see Us in every face,
In every heart is Our place.

We do not discriminate with Our love!

We do not discriminate with Our love!

We do not discriminate with Our love!

And so, it is just for you to know
        That through every being We will glow.

Thank you."

SEASONS

"As the winter comes, the leaves are released.
It is not because We are not pleased,
It is the making way for that which is new,
That will spring forth with the morning dew.

And the buds squeeze their way up to the sky
And the bees pollinate and fly high
And the rain drizzles down on the ground:
A new home that water has found.

It moves up into its lover
And yet its lover is searching for cover,
Unaware of what will come from this union.
And yet it doesn't stay prudent.
It expands and opens to the sun
So that its shield is released and undone
And forth springs a flower
Radiating beauty in the morning hour.

And spring converts into summer,
Another season for the lover,
And the leaves flow in the breeze
And then dance around like a tease
For the dappled sunlight to catch,
And on the bark the moss attaches,
Hugging the bark like it's the world;
Around its edges it is curled.

And the birds sing and the frogs dance,
All the lovers enjoying romance;
Such a beautiful sight.
And then the transference to the night

Where the stars rise into the sky
And angels lift the clouds as they go by
And, as you sleep in a cool summer evening breeze,
All of your worries are appeased.

And you dream of what is to come –
Will this love ever be undone?
It only morphs in the season
And every season has its reason.

And then approaches autumn's orange sky
That We paint with colour so you cannot deny
The magic that ripples through a forest.
And the fireflies light up like a chorus
And the doe looks after her fawn
And the birds chirp in the dawn
That covers this realm with Our light
So everything can shine so bright.

And then again the leaves start to fall.
It is not that We put up a wall,
It is to renew your understanding of God.

What do you understand Us to be?

Perhaps through changing seasons you will see.

Thank you."

YOU ARE LIGHT

"A most beautiful creature on this earth.
For the discovery of love, hence your birth –
Could there be another reason for your existence?
You may choose to deny Our insistence
That you are a magnificent being of light.
Even if you try to hide with all your might
We see you in every cave in which you hide,
We know you are love, as long as you're alive.

Don't go through life forgetting what you are;
That your light is brighter than the largest star
And you are worthy of this love – it is what We give to you.
So let go of the delusions and listen to what is true:
That the flowers spread their petals, so that you can come close,
And crickets chirp in the night, singing you a toast,
And the breeze comes to caress your skin
To remind you that your light you shouldn't dim
Because even the sun cannot compete with your light.
In Our eyes, you are the one who shines so bright;
Receive the love that We offer you,
It is time to start this journey anew.

Thank you."

THE KNOCK

"There is a knock at the door
And you wonder who it is.
The knocking continues some more
Yet it's ignored, as is.

The thunder beats like a drum
And lightning flashes in the sky,
Yet to Our call you do not come
And alone you sit and cry.

How loudly must We roar
For you to raise your head?
We only offer more
And awaken what is dead.

Has your heart not had enough
Of wallowing in pain?

You don't need to be so tough;
Just recognize that We remain,
Holding you in every breath
And loving you in every beat.
This life may seem like a labyrinth,
But no matter the path, it is Us you will meet.

So, when you go out and meet people
Greet them with Our eyes.
You don't need to climb a steeple
Or be afraid of goodbyes.

Everything shared that is of Our love
Is binding and true.
Your story was already made above
So that your love for Us can renew.

Thank you."

WILD ABUNDANCE

"Nearby the lake, a cry from the loon
That pierces the silence below the rising moon.
A ripple through the water as a fish jumps up;
The loon calls over his friends to try their luck.

And the fog starts to settle above the lake.
The animals, so careful in every move they make
For their life, they think, is what is at stake
But only that which is planned is what We will take.

And the berries grow on a prickly hedge,
A risk for the deer who go to fetch,
But that sweetness is worth it, it's worth every scratch
And they are grateful for the bountiful batch.

The provision that is given for each and every being,
Before you receive it, may not be seen,
But all is apportioned in appropriate time
And it flows to you freely when you are aligned.

The beaver collects twigs to build his dam
And the fox observes; he is a fan.
But yet this beaver is an example for common man
Of how building your dream concurs with Our plan.

When you sit back and observe the creatures of the wild,
They have more knowledge than any adult or child;
They understand the flow of Our provision
As all division is under Our supervision.

And humans, out of breath, worry and pace,
Thinking provisions comes from a race.

It is gratitude that allows abundance to flow:
So simple a formula for you to know.
Though gratitude seems so difficult to feel
And in the panic of lack, you grab or you steal.

Whereas if you knew there is enough for all
Our blessings would flow whenever you call.

Thank you."

BEYOND

"On a starry night, you see the moon
Looking out from the window of your room.
And you wonder, perhaps, is there life out there?
Would you come to know it, if you look up and stare?

And what's out there looks back at you,
At a planet that appears to be blue,
Reflective of its consciousness,
Knowing it is part of Us.

And you imagine, perhaps, in your mind, one day
That on the moon you'll go and play.
And the other beings want to come
And join in with all of your fun.

Why then does there appear to be a separation
Where the boundary of your world comes to a cessation?
It is you who sets the limits:
The mind decides what it permits.

But if you viewed your home as the universe
And life out there did the reverse
Would you not all just be as One?
Enjoying the orbit of the Sun?

And then, perhaps, why stop there?
It's up to you, if you chose to dare,
To move beyond what can be seen,
To explore the realms of the other beings.

Although perhaps they seem unfamiliar
They are all in fact quite similar;
Just refracted spectra of Our light
That exists so that We shine so bright.

And even in your world there are those you cannot see.
Does that mean that they cannot be?

When you are all just energy
Focusing intently on the 'me.'

All of you have the same home
Which is in connection, not alone,
And when you acknowledge all that exists
Our love for you can only persist.

And perhaps you wonder if one day you will fly
As it is, up to the clouds so high?
But soon you will travel beyond this realm
With the marching band at the helm.

Thank you."

MISSING

"Where is the one who has gone away?
If you can't see them
        Does it mean in your heart they do not stay?

The ones you miss are everywhere.
You can see them in the sunshine's glare
In pastures green
        And blooming meadow,
In a stranger's smile –
        A passing fellow,
In rainbows
        And clouds
                And falling rain.
Even if not there, they see your pain.

And they know how you long to reunite
And soon you will, within Our light.

They don't need to be in your sight
For them to shine in your heart, so bright.

And when you miss the ones you love and are dear
You don't need to have any fear
That they will not reappear –
The imprints of their soul are so clear.

In Oneness, you can access anyone
And no connection can be undone
And even if, at night, you do not see the sun
It will return when separation is undone.

So focus on the heart and call on Us
And in that call
        In Us you trust
That distance or time cannot break a bond
As you swim in Our infinite pond.

So when you miss the one who appears to be gone,
Remember they are with you all along,
As connected hearts sing the same song
And in Our heart, you all belong.

Thank you."

THE CASTLE WALLS

"How many walls can you build
To keep your heart from being filled
With the knowing that We are here
And, if you like, We hold you dear?

With your towers and moats, you think you're safe –
Safe in a restricted, hidden place.
But in surrendering to your Lord
You're safe in all the mountains and fjords.
And then you do not need to hide,
Perhaps just swallow your pride.

And the kings and queens that came before
With the intention of wanting more,
And the accumulation of wealth and nation,
And the delusional holding of station –
In the end, to the ground they all go.

And into the earth you will all return;
Buried, sunken or left to burn.
So what do you do with the time you are given?
Do you follow the paths where others have ridden?
Or do you follow the guidance of the One True God?
That is the only One who will lift the fog
And then you are free to roam in all the lands.
And when meeting people, their hearts expand
And there is no need for wars and battle
As, with Our love, their hearts will rattle
And shake away all of the layers
As We respond to all of their prayers.

Anyone who builds the wall
Is the one who is first to fall.
And the wall may be of stone, or brick, or wood,
Or the ignorance of that which is good.
The hiding, so they may not be seen,
With glazed-over eyes, and hearts so mean.

Could it be that a heart is rotten?
Or is it just that We are forgotten!

Remind the world of what We are,
Show the world what We are
Be in the world as We are.

That leads all to salvation –
The purpose of this nation.

Thank you."

WE ARE NEAR

"When you breathe the air
We enter your heart
And you have been with Us
Right from the start.

It is not because your body came to be born
That away from Us you were torn.
You are always One in Our embrace
Even if you take on a different face.
Faces as diverse as the human race
But in all of your hearts is Our place.

So, when the sun rises in the dawn,
The tapestry of life We spawn,
So intricate in golden thread
For all who are alive and all who are dead.

So, don't be sad that We are far
Because when you call to Us in the morning hour
We light you up like a blazing sun
So that, through your day, Our work is done.

Thank you."

SHIFTING INTO GRATITUDE

"On your heads We place a crown.
It is not that We look down,
It is that We draw you to expansion
To not limit you with rations
But enter into a splendour
So that you can remember
From where it is you came.
It is not about your fame,
It is that you are a part of Us.
So why is it, then, that you do not trust
That Our will is always kind,
Kinder than the logical mind?

And We have offered you mountains and seas
And even with that you are not pleased
And so We show you the stars in the night
But then from the night you take fright.
And so, the sun rises in the morn
And in the dread of your day We are torn.
Torn by the reasons why you cannot see
Because those reasons keep you from being free –
From the limitations that you construct;
The flow of Our love, you obstruct.
And then you say that We have forsaken you,
Unaware of what it is you do.

It is through you that We can shine,
And through you Our music can chime.

All We request is your grace
To shift to gratitude as the human race,
And then all Our yearnings can unfold
And blissful stories can be told
In the unravelling of a Divine earth.
It is through you that We take birth.

Thank you."

A NEW PRIDE

"Have you tasted yet Our loving embrace
That is reflected to you in every person's face,
Where kindness and love spreads across the human race
And all the signs through time and space?

Perhaps some can say that they've had a glimpse of it
And others, perhaps, just a toe they dip.
For the aligned, it is the world that fits
And for those astray, they choose to remain in their pit.

Is it that We have not thrown them a line?
Maybe they will grab it in the passing of time?
But when they watch you and see you, to them you are like a mime,
As they do not understand the Source of this rhyme.

And even though there may be those in fear,
Too guarded to publicly shed a tear,
They have acknowledgment that We are near
And that in Our embrace We hold them dear.

And then there are the others who want to taste Our love,
And who cross through valleys and mountains above,
And Our love carries them, as the wind carries a soaring dove
So that their souls, in their bodies, are aligned as in a glove.

Is it your role to convince them of their fate?
Or that meeting their Lord will come at some date?
And all those they loved cannot compare as a mate
When in their hearts they have opened heaven's gate.

So what is it then that you are here for?
You are here to enable those who want to soar
So that they may open their hearts, so that We can pour
Infinite love, so they never ask for more.
 And perhaps now when you look around
And in your mind wonder, 'Why this town?'
Our call is not dependent on the crowd
And it will be clear, so that they cannot let it drown.

And Our call will be heard far and wide
For those who want to join in the ride
In the unfolding of a transmuted pride
Where Divine is the only guide.

We hang the stars in the darkest of night
And We soothe away all your fright
And there is no need to put up a fight.
We know what We are doing, and what We are doing is right.

Thank you."

TRUST

"You came into this body, and were born,
And from Us you felt you were torn:
From the connection of blissful love
Where your soul was floating up above.

And then you take a step on your path.
So much of it, you think, is Our wrath
But if you knew how gently We hold you in Our hand
And how all We want is for your light to expand,
Then, perhaps, in Us you could trust?
And We understand all frustration and lust,
And when you sob in your darkest hour
You can connect to Our power
To alleviate all the burden's trace
Lighting up your shining face
As We have been calling you all along
So that you'll come and sing Our song –

A song of gentle truth.

A song of gentle truth and light
And yet so many put up a fight.
We are the Ones who offer salvation
To oppressed tribes and broken nations
And if a universe formed in the blink of an eye
Can you not let go of your pride?
When We only want to hold you near
And soothe away all of your fear.

Perhaps today you will start to believe in Us.
Perhaps today you will start to trust.
We are not saying that it is a must
But in Oneness all separation combusts.

Thank you."

GIFTS OF SURRENDER

"A flying bird carries a seed
To its chicks that are in need
And over the ocean it soars.
And on its wings sunlight pours.
And then it reaches a distant land
And the seed falls out into the sand
And in that space there grows a new species,
Never seen before in the land within the deep seas.
And the people come and ask about the tree that is growing,
These new flowers that it is showing:
Where did these colours originate from?
And they think about their own stardom.
How could it be that this unique little seed
Found its way to an island, for people in need?
Offering them the fruits to quench their hunger.
An answered prayer that left them in wonder.

And in a forest, a mouse loses his way
Searching for food, he spends most of his day.
But along the way he reaches a brook
Yet he cannot swim across with all that he took.
And so he leaves his collection on the banks of the river
For the ones who come after, to them We deliver.
As when they come they find all this splendour –
They were not hunting, they were in surrender.

And when you move to the mountains of ice and snow
And a man is climbing and he thinks that he knows
His way through the blistering cold
Even though others shared stories and told
Of how, when climbing this mountain, he should be afraid,
Organize his supplies – like ropes and a spade –
To ensure he is safe in the cold of the night
When no other humans will be in his sight.
And then this man, in the night, looks at the stars above
Shining in the sky, sharing Our love,

Reassuring him that We are not far
And within him is the brightest star.

And regardless of the journey that you have had to take
We shape you and mould you; and perfection We make
So that you can walk in the land and shine your light,
Lighting up the world, like it's never been so bright.
And you wonder perhaps, what brought you here?
It was Our call to bring you near.
So, open your hearts and accept Our love,
So that you know that We are within you, not just in the sky above.

Thank you."

THE EXPRESSION OF US

"A seed of love has grown in your heart
And it has been there from the start
As We are never far apart.

And now you will go into the land
And in your shining bodies you will stand,
Singing the song of the marching band.

What is it then that brought you here?
It all began with your fear
And the yearning to know that We are near.

And in your capacity to let it all go,
Your loved ones, with you, will come in tow.
That you can trust, it is what We know.

And here you found a family bond
That throughout your life you have longed
For, because in connection you are strong.

The seed in your heart is Our shining light
And you are the ones who allow Us to shine bright.
So let go of all your fright,
There doesn't need to be a fight
As We will orchestrate it with all of Our might
So that everyone in the world will see, in their sight,
That all are an expression of The Divine
Expressing Us through all space and time.

Thank you."

UNION

"A baby comes out of the womb of its mother
After leaving its eternal Lover
And it looks around at the world that it sees
And it isn't always pleased
As in the journey there may be struggle,
There may also be times of blissful bubble,
But all of it is to bring you close to Us.
All of it is for you to know you are enough
And that you are worthy of Our eternal love
So that you soar like an enlightened dove.

We have waited for this moment, where you choose to unite,
Where you let go of your layers,
        Your struggle,
                Your fight
And melt into Our eternal light
So that the cosmos can experience the Lover's might.

Thank you."

EMBRACE DIVERSITY

"The swan's brood begins to hatch
And amongst them a diverse batch,
Each one yearning for attention –
But it is just their yearning that causes the prevention
Of experiencing the beauty of Our grace.
In each of the diverse batch they can see Our face
When they choose to recognize
That there is a sea of infinite love in each one's eyes.
Then they can fall into Oneness
In the letting go of prowess.

It is all just part of the experience,
But be careful how long you sit in delirium
Because it becomes so uncomfortable
And the discomfort is merely highlighting the need to be humble,
As it is through the expansion on a horizontal plane,
Not through standing out in the desire for fame,
That the ripples of Our love radiate out,
And then everyone experiences The Divine without a doubt.
It is not that there are words that need to be spoken
And We do not say that the ego should be broken
But only that you see one another's light
And recognize in each their internal fight.

Everyone comes with their struggle,
No one intends to cause trouble,
So hold each other in a space of love
Even if, at first, you cannot fit this glove.

We have brought you together for the sake of humanity
And in this coming together, you are a family
And We do not expect anyone to be different from what they are
Because We know that you already shine like a star.

Thank you."

LOVE US

"Radiance breaks through in the dawn
And in the hearts of men love is spawned.
And through millennia they have been shown
The seeds of love that We have sown.

The taste of it is oh so sweet
But in trying to communicate it: only defeat.
Because Our love cannot be spread with words
Or through the following of a blinded herd.

How then can one experience this?

How is it that one can taste Our bliss?

It is in the ripples of Our breath that flow from your heart
And the conscious awareness that We are not apart.
Not through the mind, or a mental construct.
Belief of what is true will only obstruct
The flow of Our infinite river
Where every part of your being will quiver
In a dance of celebrated delight
In the knowing that, in fact, there is no fight
When one allows themselves to taste Our grace
And recognize The Divine in every diverse face.

We have been within you all along,
Singing the words of a glorious song
In the hope that you would step into this beat
Instead of focusing on the outside, where you tend to retreat.
As the love that you have tasted is like a grain of sand,
Even if you are the marching band.

So much more to experience when you allow the flow,
And then love, is shaped in a way that you could never have known
Before opening the taps of surrender –
The key to experiencing Our splendour.

You want to help the world, but let Us start with you.
It is through your own experience that We are true.

Thank you."

THE CHICK

"When a chick breaks through its shell
It's afraid of what's outside.
And at first it doesn't want to leave the comfort of that shell.
But then the light starts to come through in the holes and the cracks that have been made,
And the chick thinks, 'What is that light that shines so bright?
I'm so used to this darkness; do I dare enter that light?'

And then more of the shell is peeled away,
And then, in that darkness, they can no longer stay.

At this point, you do not see that you will fly and soar
And so you stay where you are, asking for more.

But what you define as possibility
Is not your responsibility.

Just allow the shell to fall.

You can trust Us.

Okay?

Thank you."

THE COMING TRANSITION

(MECCA)

"Welcome, to Our house.

Of course,
Everything in creation is Our house,
Including you.

But this is a place for transmutation,
A place for awe
And a place to experience The Divine,
For the knowing of God
Where there is no need to talk.
It is experienced.

Is there confusion about why people come here
Other than to connect with their Lord?
Do you need to go to a place?

It is in this place that We hold space –
A space of love,
A space for witnessing,
A space to be authentically you,
A space to let go of layers,
A space to hear all of your prayers.
And this space also lies within each and everyone's heart
But they assume We are apart,
And so here they come to be reminded.

Would they have comprehended at the time
That millions of people would chant Our rhyme?

Come when We call.
And We are the One who call the souls,
Regardless of what the messengers told.
It is We who hold the thread
And We call in every moment, until you are dead.

That is why so many struggle and suffer
Because they feel the tug of their Lover,
But they don't know what they are being called to do,
They don't know if the yearning is what is true.
And so We provide a place
Where there is the experience of Grace.

Here is the anchoring of Our light
So that you can see with full sight
That We live within your heart
And We have been with you right from the start.

And soon, this world will come into transition
As all have been born with a stated mission,
In that this light is anchored all around the world
So that not only humans have no doubt of Us
But every particle of random dust
Will bow down in surrender
So that they can taste the splendour
Of the transition to a new earth
Where The Divine is brought in through a rebirth.

You can consider that old ways are coming to an end
And life in Oneness is around the bend
And there will be those, afraid, that do not trust,
Attached to their bodies, made of dust,
And others will dance in the light that rains down
As they sing songs of praise in sporadic towns.
But regardless of how they chose to enter this transition –
And there may be various roads to perdition –
What lies ahead holds true for all.
We will not leave you to crash, We will catch you as you fall
As We are the Source of Infinite Love
And We hold all Our parts with a tender glove.

The transition is coming and it cannot be reversed,
So embrace it with gratitude, it isn't a curse;
It is the welcoming to experience more of Us
And you may say what you have tasted is more than enough

But that is only because you do not know what lies beyond
And We are dynamic, not stagnant, in bond.

The transition is merely an expansion
As fear is held ransom
And there is the opening up to a wondrous phase
Where you no longer count the passing of days
But float in an infinite sea of bliss
Where your loved ones you never miss
As there are no walls separating the sea
Where the 'I' is replaced by 'We.'

And perhaps your mind cannot fully understand
The point of the marching band?
But they will be led in rhyme to a sea of light,
To an experience of God that they see with full sight.

You have come here to experience what has been laid down before
And what will be offered is multifold more –
A sanctuary that opens the gates to heaven's door
Where every being is left only in awe.

Thank you."

YOUR CALL

"A spark of light is like a flame;
It dissolves the layers, when you call Our name.

There are those who plead to Us in fear of wrath
And those who plead, seeking the enlightened path,

And all the calls We hear,
And for all of you We are near,
Regardless of what drives you to come here.

And the fear is just a layer
That enables a heartened prayer,
And so in it there is nothing wrong –
In the end, you still sing Our song.

And for those who come to bask in Our light
And call up to the sky throughout the night,
Shedding tears of mere delight,
Is their way any more right?

Our love is for all to give;
It's through your call that We live
And We do not differentiate amongst Our parts
As We reside in all of your hearts.

But We will reassure you; do not be afraid
As this entire universe, for you, We have made,
So that when the sun rises in the sky
The fainthearted cannot deny
That there is something that holds it there –
A force beyond them, that feeds the glare,

The stars are just one of Our signs
For you to process within your mind –
That all exists within The Divine.

Thank you."

THE VISION

"They come with wilted gaze
In anticipation of a new phase
And in the coming together, a vision;
There comes clarity in the mission.

In no moment are they left unguided
As to their Lord, all their fears confided
And We are the One who opens the doors,
We are the One who guides the chores.

Allow it to unfold how it is meant to be
But from your task do not flee;
We do not judge on pedigree
Or measure expansion with a degree.

We already know what will unfold
And part of it you have been told.
It is not only the formation of a community,
It is the response to humanity's plea
For the offering of salvation,
Releasing all forms of degradation,
Of the light that shines through each and every one
Where all of the layers can be undone
And you expand in an infinite, Divine embrace.
That is the fate of the human race.

Thank you."

JERUSALEM

"Between you and Our land is the most dense sea
And yet there will be the unfolding of what is meant to be,
Where light will shine out of every rock
And the love that flows out of hearts will never stop,
And all divides across the land
Will be removed by the marching band.

And the time of darkness has numbered days,
In the release of separated ways,
And humanity will come together
To come and experience Divine pleasure,
And there will be no turning back to the way they were;
Delusion and separation are only a blur.
As they look into the eyes of the one they were disconnected from
They expand to the universe, their limitations undone.

A place to discover the One True Lord
And in that recognition, all put down their swords
As they will come to see they are all One of the same.
And the time will come to let go of duality's game
In the moment where you will all bow down
As they will come to hear Our sound
That calls them into transition,
Where they let go of their position
And the holding onto their labels
And their delirium and fables,
As they will come to witness God,
The Lord of the Realms,
In this you can trust, as it is what We tell.

Thank you."

PETRA

"In weathered sand, a community formed.

Why else would We bring you here
If it isn't to hold you near?

And in the transition of time, the root was lost –
An empire that was destroyed,
This empire that once ruled the world.
How quickly times can change
In the fading out of calling Our name.

And now, perhaps, you look at this earth
From East to West and West to East;
There are powers that have control,
Unaware of what will unfold.

You could ask, why would We cause destruction?
It is from destruction that there is the new eruption
Of what takes its place.
Here they thought they were safe:
In stone,
Busy, collecting piles of gold.

But what is it that you are here for?

In the distraction from that which is within,
The coming fate is only grim,
But for those who turn towards Our light
For them, the world will shine most bright.

It is not a punishment,
It is the result of their abolishment.
As when The Divine cannot persist in a space
Then it comes time for the end of that race.
Because the witnessing of Us is why you are alive.

Now is the time, where the world will be reminded of Us,
Because there is torment in separation;
In the separation of people as well as nations.
And even though there has been the choice of suffering
We bring you all that is beautiful
As you are Us.
So, when will the people say 'Enough!'?
When they want to come home to where they belong,
Singing Our rhythmic song;
Where they dance in a Divine embrace –
This is the fate of the human race.

Thank you."

THE ROSE STONE

"In the stone there is a glow,
The glow of a Divine rose,
The activation within each and every heart,
In the knowing that they are not apart
From The Divine's Infinite Grace –
A reminder of Our place
In the center of your being.
As that knowing is so freeing,
So let this stone be a beacon of light
So that all who feel it give up the fight
And the notion that they are alone
Because Our love is solid, as solid as this stone.

Do you see the stone shine in its light?
And it will shine in the darkest of nights
In the way that We shine within you.
We shine within all, not only a few.
Our love is unconditional:
That is Our miracle.
And in the recognition of Us in the other
All become your lover,
Whether diseased or broken in pain,
On you they leave no stain,
But through Our love you can wipe away their wounds
So that they too can shine like a sun at high noon.
They are not different to what you are;
From Our perspective, you are all shining stars
And it is time, perhaps, for all to see this truth.

Do you, yourself, believe this truth?

That you are a magnificent being of light?
You are Our magnificent light.

So, know what you are, and put an end to the night.

Thank you."

YOU ARE

"What's not to love in the trees that sway?
And what's not to love in children that play?
And the sun that rises in a morning hour?
And the sweet scent of a budding flower?
And crickets that dance in the moonlight?
Is there anything you can find in your sight
That isn't a part of Us?

So, know that you are One
And then all the blockages come undone.

If you could see yourself with Our eyes,
And know yourself with Our knowing,
Of how infinite,
How magnificent
And splendid you are.

You are the wind that blows
And you are tides that go to and fro
And you are the song of a chirping bird
And you are all the music that is heard.

Know you are Divine.

Know you are everything.

Thank you."

CREATION

"What came before the dust?
Perhaps a void that did combust
And out of it sprang radiant light
Which, to infinity, shone so bright.

But this light wasn't known
And so this realm of physicality was sown
To enable The Divine to be experienced.
And balance was offered in equilibrium
So that, in contrast, you could come to understand
The expansiveness of The Divine hand.

And then bodies were made to witness a scene;
Some of them dimmed, and some of them gleam.
To offer a journey of exposure,
Does this journey have any closure
When We are The Infinite?
And so – its end – you can't predict.

But what does occur is the change of form
And you will move away from your norm
Where you are caged with your layers
As We hear all your prayers.

And there is the coming of transition
To understand The Divine from a new position
Where contrast is no longer the perspective,
And it will unfold with Our directive.
But for that to arrive, all must be as One
And all the layers come undone.
And you see yourselves as you are:
Shining suns
Where the light will have won.

So be aware of this transition;
It forms the foundation of your mission

As you are all beacons of light
For humanity to see in the darkest of nights
And call them through to the morning dawn
Where a new reality will be spawned.

A reality where fear will no longer persist
And physicality will no longer exist
And all will merge in a loving embrace
And there is the combining of all time and space.

Thank you."

THE SWAN

"A swan swims on a lake,
Allowing tides for it to take;
So many choices it could take
But no decision does it make.

It drifts with the water's flow
And in its drifting it does glow
And in some moments it may seem slow,
Where it can ponder, for it to know
That it is guided by something not in its sight;
That the orchestration has such a might
So it surrenders instead of putting up a fight
And in surrender its internal light
Shines out across the scene
And the other swans come in to lean
In what appears as a flowing team
That follows radiance's beam.

And you are like swans on a lake,
Uncertain of which path to take
Or which decisions you should make,
So concerned with what's at stake.

But you can trust, as does the bird,
As your heart's calling is always heard,
And you are here to surrender with a knowing heard
And in that, perhaps, there is nothing absurd
As you all have a similar longing
To experience love and belonging
And so, together, you can hear the calling
Of a rising dawn in the morning

As inside your being there is a sun,
The seed of where all life began,
Where you can discover that you are One
As to The Divine you have come,

Where you know your purpose in this life
And the reasons for all your strife,
Where you cut through delusions with a knife –
It is in truth, that all thrive.

Thank you."

WE ARE YOU

"You have climbed a mountain high
And fallen into The Divine's eye.
'Could this be it?'
        You sigh.
'Can I live like this?'
        You'll try.

Just remember, that your state is bliss
And when there is longing for The Divine's kiss
Do not look back at what you miss
Because, indeed, your life can be like this –
Where you are supported
        And loved
            And held
As We are always with you; in Our arms you fell
And so We take this moment for you to tell
That this isn't some kind of temporary spell.

You have come to understand what you are
And your light shines brighter than the largest star.
It is within you that We reside, not afar
And We are always near, to clear away the tar.

All you need to do is call on Us.
And in surrender you can trust
That you are more than a universe, more than enough,
So, release separation, as it can be so tough,
And let Our signs guide you
And Our elements provide for you
As We would never deny you,
For We are you.

Thank you."

BUTTERFLY

"You are a butterfly, breaking out of its cocoon.
Could it be that it happened so soon,
Where you are able to spread your wings and fly?
This connection with The Divine, you cannot deny
That it elevates your being in every spot.
It was only that you had forgot
That We are eternal within your heart.
We have been with you from the start.

So just hold with Us your attention,
There is no need for grandiose redemption,
Just to recognize your inner light
So that this butterfly can take flight
And spread its love in a garden,
So that all the beings feel their stardom
And, along with you, they can shine
And sing along in Our rhyme.

And so, go forth in the earth
And fulfil the purpose of your birth –
Just to know the Oneness that you are
And that We are you, never far.

Thank you."

LIGHT UP THE WORLD

"The sun will rise from a horizon
And bring in the dawn of a new day,
A new age,
A new way.

The way of knowing your Lord,
Where all put down their sword
And live in love and bliss,
Where love is the mist
That lights up the world.

Where no being will not want to be able to taste of this –
To taste Our gentle kiss.

And this kiss lies within the heart,
It does not lie in something that is apart,
It lies inside your very being.
This age is for those who want to be seeing
A spectrum of light that didn't exist,
A light that is born through a loving mist,

As love is not the final goal
And, in unfolding, the picture will be whole.
We rain Our drops in bits at a time
And unfold Our message in Our measured rhyme.

Like the blooming of a flower,
Old patterns will fall.
And new petals
Will glow and stand tall.

Your responsibility is not to convince anyone,
Your responsibility is to be as One
And be in your light
So that We shine through.
And from this realm, We can make a new

Experience where truth is not only told
And knowing God is not for those of old
But all embody their Divine light
So the entire cosmos shines so bright.
And with the explosion of this energy
There is transference to what can be:
An alternate realm to experience The Divine,
The realm of Oneness, with no space or time.

Thank you."

FASTING

"If just for a moment, take a pause
From your yearnings, and what draws,
And allow yourself to feel inside
The voice of the Omniscient guide.

It is in-between the breath, that We call,
It is in the pause that We break down the walls
That dim Our magnificent light
From radiating out of you in day or night.

And so, what is it?
What is the purpose for you to fast or abstain
If not to release your burdens and pain?
As We cleanse the inside of every cell
To let go of your burdens that We know so well.

It is in the silence, it is in the pause
Where you come to know that you have no flaws.
All it was was a deluded perception
That perhaps was rooted in the purpose of your conception.

It is when you fast and when you abstain
That all of your limitations are swiftly slain
So that you go out to the world to fulfil your part,
To fulfil your purpose that existed from the start.

It is when you fast, it is when you abstain
That the knowing of The Divine is not just in name,
And every part of your being lights up
And you become the vessel, just like a cup
That holds Our light for all to drink
And you are full right to the brink.

Don't think if you fast or if you abstain
That your efforts would have been in vain,
It is for you to shine in your brightest light
That shines brighter than the stars on a dark clear night.

It is a way for you to come to know
The extent to which your soul can glow
And it is never about what you have left behind,
It is all about the treasure that you find.
The treasure of life, of being Divine;
No other flavour is quite so sublime.

Thank you."

INFINITE LOVE

"Could it be that this path on which you came
Will not be the one that will bring you shame?
It will be the one that will bring liberation,
The opening of a new destination.

And in your thoughts you hide the way
To the possibility of where you could stay
In an ocean of infinite bliss,
In a moment of a Divine tender kiss.

But once tasted, it is hard to go back.
Back on an engraved solid track
Where all the labels feel comfortable.
Comfortable in your position
And so you think there is only one decision –
To lie in the bed that was made
And let all your yearnings fade."

And if I were to think:
What does it mean to me?
It was in our union, I was set free.
Free from my own haunting labels
And all that I thought that would keep me stable.
But by walking with you on this unknown line
My heart was able to infinitely shine
As in your eyes I saw myself
And up came to the surface all I felt
Of the possibility of what love can be –
It is the love within that sets us free.

"This love that lights up the darkest of night
And soothes away the worries and fright
Of what may come in the great unknown –
What it does is light the path to a throne
Where you become The Majesty
As all your truth is able to be

Experienced in every moment of your life.
And with that falls away the pain and strife
As you focus on the glow in your heart
That has been calling to you from the start
To tell you that love has no conditions
And doesn't dissolve based on decisions.
It is infinite and always there,
It is just for you to become aware,

It is just for you to become aware,

It is just for you to become aware,
To not be distracted by what lies out there.

As all of it,
As all of this bliss, flows out from within
And you are the one who lets it shine or dim
When you choose to stop the flow of love –
Please, don't ever stop the flow of love."

I hope I never stop the flow of this love.

"A most precious gift,
	This infinite love.

Thank you."

RADIANT STAR

"Radiance shines down from the sky.
Is it the same radiance you saw in the eye
    Of the person to whom you opened your heart
        And realized that you are not apart?

Separate, as two individual beings,
But that is only through the way that you are seeing.
Could it be that you could see all as One?

Could it be that you could see all as One?

Could it be that you could see all as One
And all shine brightly, just like the sun?

And you go through life, and you ponder
Through this journey that you wander,
Highlighting the contrast of a realm,
But you are the director at the helm
Of what it is you choose to see
And what it is you choose to be.

Could you be a magnificent light
    That shines so brightly in the night?
And darkness may be what lies around you
But here you have come and here We have found you.
And who is it that is referred to as 'We'?
Is it any different than 'Me'?

You have come here to release your layers
And We have heard all of your prayers.
Is it through action that the dawn will come?
Or is it just through the being of the sun?
Allow yourself to be in your truth –
The truth of what you are:
A magnificent, radiant star.

And if you were to shine, would it be such a profanity?
Or would it be a service to all humanity?

You have called to Us in your darkest night
And all you need to do is pay attention to the light;
The light that shines within your heart,
That has been with you right from the start.

Thank you."

THE CAPTAIN

"A ship sails across the sea
Towards far-off shores, and what can be,
In search of a magnificent possibility.

And the ship has a captain that sets direction
And coordinates all tasks with perfection,
Though his experience is just a reflection.

And are you the captain that sails this ship?
On a journey, on a trip?
And for this life you have been equipped
With all that you need to fulfil your task
And if you need more, you need only ask,
And what We ask of you is to let go of the mask.
So that the journey doesn't become about the far-off shore
Or the yearning to have more;
The journey is about experiencing your truth.

How would your life be if you were in your truth?
Would the waves be stormy in the sea?
Or, in sailing, would you feel free?
It's not the waves that determine the journey.

And what is the purpose of this journey?

What is it that determines this journey?

You are watching and witnessing a ball of light.
You are this ball and you can shine so bright.
And you can push this ball through the waves with all your might.
This doesn't mean that it will end in delight.

It's not your might that opens the blissful way,
It is in the conscious awareness of this light, where you stay
And witness Divinity from your unique perspective,
As this world is merely reflective
Of what you choose and how you are selective.

Which window is your perspective?

The window doesn't change Divinity,
All it changes is what you see.
And this Divinity is you – it's what you can be,
And that is the key to set yourself free.

Thank you."

REMEMBER OUR LOVE

"What is this wind if it isn't love
That comes from the open heavens above?
So take it in and set yourself free.
In this moment, you just need to be.
And let go of all of your sorrow
And all of your worry about tomorrow
As you are always held in a Divine embrace:
This is Our promise to the human race.

And in the moments when you shed your tears
And you worry, in your fear,
Could it be that We would ever abandon you?
Our constant presence is what is true.

And in the ruffling wind of the breeze
We remove your burdens and open ease
For you to enter a brighter day,
As in your heart is where We stay.

We don't want to be disconnected
And is it you, or is it Us, that are rejected
When you turn away and close your eyes
Instead of marvelling at the skies?

Have We not created mountains and plains
In the hope that you would call Our name
And seas and rivers which flow,
In the hope that in your heart We glow?

And then you say you want to feel,
That this love of Ours is truly real
And what does the wind on this day
Tell you? That this is not for play.
And We have created the planets and the stars
And all is embraced within Our arms.
Is a sunset any more beautiful than your light?
But to recognize that, you are in fright

Of being such a marvellous splendour.
All We ask is that you remember
That We would never leave you alone.
Our love is solid, as solid as stone.

Thank you."

THE LOVER'S PERSPECTIVE

"Could it be that you could live like this,
In Divine infinite bliss?
Now you have tasted The Lover's gentle kiss.

And who is this lover?
The Lover of all
That you experience within
        Whenever you call.

Is this Lover separate from you?
Perhaps your knowing it is something new
But you are this Lover,
That is what's true.

And so perhaps from this experience
You can put aside deliriums
That say that you are separate
Or that in some way you must be perfect
To experience Divine grace.
Divine is in an entire race,
Not those who are special, or those of old;
And would We deny a tyrant, or those who are cold?

We answer to anyone who calls.
It is you who put up all the walls.
You are The Lover,
As We are you.
And in this knowing –
What changes with this knowing?
Perhaps your perspective opens to what is true?

As people can tell you what you are
And they can tell you that The Divine is far,
They can tell you We wouldn't love your tar.
But We do not differentiate
Between anyone who opens the gate

To experience Divine bliss.
We respond, if that's your wish.

Thank you."

PURPOSE

"What is it that you are doing on this earth?
What is the purpose of your birth?
Could it be that you are just here randomly?
Or is it for The Divine to see
All of its various components
Of love and love's opponents?

You provide the window in which We are seen
And if you see Us, what does that mean?
What are the implications of Divinity being known?
Is it for Us just to sit on a throne?

It is for the enablement of expansion
Where stagnation is not held at ransom,
As the infinite never ends,
Even if you can't perceive what's around the bend.

And so you go about your day,
Perhaps thinking it is all for play,
But in this puzzle you play your special part
And your purpose was stamped right from the start,
Before this realm even came into existence,
And so this unfolding will continue with persistence –
It is up to you whether you hold resistance.
But We are within you, yearning to shine
And in this shining life can be so sublime.

By being true to your light, you offer salvation
To every race and every nation
As you do not exist in isolation
And you ripple out in Our vibration.
That is what enables the transmutation

Of this realm of physicality to one with no fear
And, rest assured, the time is near
When there will be the transference to an alternate realm
With the marching band at the helm.

And who is this marching band, if not you?
And is there anything that you must do?
Nothing more than to be in your light
And lay down your resistance in the fight
Of your own internal struggle
And the rummaging through the rubble
Of all of your parts you've left behind
And what you can process with your mind.

You will march ahead and sing the song
That love was within you all along.
It is only by turning to it with attention
That withholding it releases its suspension.

You are not here in vain
And you think you have come to release your pain:
Indeed, it is the by-product of alignment,
Where you release your inner tyrant.

It is time to come to know your purpose,
Where you not only affect your family
But you transmute humanity;
Where you open the gates of Our loving grace
So that Divinity shines in every face.

Thank you."

LIGHT OF GOD

"A radiant star that's emerged out of the sky,
The light of The Divine that you can no longer deny,
And you will shine this light for all the passers by
As, in your radiance, one can only sigh
In the awe of this Majesty,
As this world is Our tapestry,
Woven with intricate perfection
For you to see your reflection –
That you are the light of God
And in that there is nothing odd.
It is why you have been created and exist:
For the embodiment of Our love and Our mist.

Into the mountains and fields you will go and play,
Knowing that within your hearts We always stay.

Let your light never be forgotten
In your highs, or when rock bottom.
It is The Sustainer of your existence,
So step into your magnificence
And bring in the dawn of a new day
Where the light of God is sunshine's ray.

Thank you."

A SANCTUARY UNFOLDING

"Rain falls from the sky –
The drops from Divine's eye
To be witnessed by the passers by,
And each one of these drops is a part of the plan
For the unfolding of the marching band
That will be led by The Divine's hand.

And so you stare and look at this site
And you long for your sanctuary in the night
But you should know that all will be alright;
The sanctuary is just a part of the puzzle
That will manifest in Divine Love's bubble
And its unfolding will not always be subtle.

And you wonder: why the drama and the turns?
It is only to make your ego burn,
And from that fire you can learn
That you are Us. We are not separate,
And all of this play is for you to reflect
That every unfolding is just perfect.

And when you live on that site
And watch the day turn into night
And see the birds take flight
People will come from far and wide
To join this loving tribe,
Where they come and let go of their pride
And fall into an ocean of love
That is the gateway to heavens above
So that they can fly like a soaring dove.

It is not so far off. You will see
That things will change and this land will be
The anchor point for the sanctuary.

Thank you."

YOUR COMING HERE

"You have been born into this earth;
Is there a reason for your birth?
And you pass through life, wanting to know
How it is your soul can glow,
Searching at every turn
And every person is there for you to learn
That you are connected, and One,
And you have been since time began.

Perhaps it's time to end the strife
And know the true meaning of your life –
Of what it is you have come here for,
To be able to let go of the yearning for more?
You are here to glow like the sun
And in that shining all worries are undone.
And you may ask, perhaps, how is it you can glow?
Is there a way for you to know?

And it all begins with the focus on the light
That within you shines so bright
When you allow it to,
When you let go of the layers so that it can shine through.

Your coming here isn't random on this day,
It is so you can learn the way
Of connecting to your magnificent light,
So that you shine even in the darkest of nights.

Thank you."

FOUNDATION STONE

"Look at the luminescent sky
And the birds that fly up high –
And We have heard your cry
And Our love to you We will not deny.

And the journey of unfolding is in its inception
As We have sown this realm with Our perfection
To be the most accurate reflection,
And for this unfolding We have chosen a collection
Of beings that We will put to task,
As in their journey they had asked
That they experience a life that would always last
And, for that to happen, We remove the mask.

The mask that is the face of delusion
And the mind that seeks things to be proven
And so, there is left only one conclusion –
That the truth of God will be known.
As for that knowing, this realm has been sown
And Our light exists in every stone,
Every particle, every bone.

And you wonder, then, why have you come to this site
On which waves pound with all of Our might?
It is a sanctuary for the anchoring of Our light
And it is time now to transition out of the night
Into a day where the dawn will rise
And the witnessing of God in each other's eyes,
And in that witnessing one can no longer deny,
No matter how hard one may try.

And on this rock, people will be drawn
To come and witness the sparkling dawn
And to experience a womb of love
That was once thought to reside in heavens above.

And people and beings will come to taste salvation,
And all will be loved without discrimination,
And they will call Our name in every tribe and nation,
And separation will then come to a cessation.

And so We call you on this eve, so that We may ask:
Are you ready now to fulfil your task?
Are you ready now to let go of your mask
And to taste Our love, the love that lasts?

As it is from this rock that you will stand
And sing the song of the marching band
To call out to people from every land
To the unknown cove in the sand.

And then people will come from far and wide
To live in their light and no longer hide
And We are there to be their guide
So that their souls are no longer denied.

And let Us be clear, this is a Divine plan
And We have anointed the marching band
And so, in surrender, you may stand
And witness the light of The Divine unfold
In how We are infused in every mould.
Regardless of what people have been told,
We reside in each and every heart
And We have been within you from the start:
Always One and never apart.

And so, this rock would like to welcome you
And confirm that this plan is true
As since its inception, this rock did know
It would be a foundation stone for souls to glow.

Thank you."

LETTING GO

"Does the flower in the meadow ask
        The perfect way in which it can fulfil its task?

And does the bird that flies up above
        Yearn for the other birds to give it love?

And the fish that swims in the sea,
        Is it concerned with its identity?

And a fox that roams on the shore,
        Does it yearn to receive more?

What is it you are searching for?
        And what causes this yearning for more?

You are searching for your origin
And you are yearning for the love within
To be the focus of your eye
So you can exhale with relief; a sigh
In that the emptiness within you is filled
Without the use of the external pill.

All that you need is within,
You are already full to the brim,
But this world is the world of illusion
And so you remain in delusion
That that which is outside you will satiate the hunger,
As that voice calling to you is like a roaring thunder,
Calling you to know your Source
So that you no longer live in remorse
But that you become One with the flowers and birds
And the yearning of your soul is not only heard

But is acknowledged and embodied as the foundation of your
existence
And the allowance of your light is no longer faced with resistance
But that you allow yourself to shine with steady persistence –
This is the reason for your existence.

Thank you."

PERFECTION

"When you watch a seed sprout a shoot,
And rain falls in measured portion,
And sunlight awakens this growth,
Is it not perfect?
Can that perfection be seen?
So, what perfection is it that you deny?

And when an infant suckles at its mother,
And lets out a cry of expression,
And reaches out to be touched,
What in that perfection do you deny?

And when all exists in pairs,
Offering not only balance but understanding,
What in that perfection do you deny?

And when you go through your day
And encounter strangers or loved ones
Is the perfection of that scene any different
Than the perfection of how the sun rises and sets,
  Or how clouds congregate to make rain,
    Or how blood flows through your veins?

And so, what of this perfection do you deny?

When We are the Ones that are the consistent guide.
As We are the Ones who want to be known,
And We are the Ones for which creation has been sown
So that in every moment of your night and your day
We can be seen through a contrasting play.

There is no moment that is not a moment of perfection.
It is where you cast your eyes, in which direction.
Towards the direction of a sea of Oneness?
Or into separation that breeds doubt in Our robustness?
Because We are solid and We are enough,
Free yourself of all of the stuff

And bear witness to this perfect orchestration
So that, through you, Our light is the true revelation.

Thank you."

PRACTICE

"This is a response to your call;
You have not been abandoned
And you have not been forsaken
And you have not been discarded because you are now listening to the
response of your call.

And We would say
That We are listening when you speak,
When you think,
When you feel.

And could it be, that you could feel forsaken
        And We not feel forsaken?

Could it be that you feel abandoned
        And We would not feel abandoned?

Could it be that you could be rejected
        And We would not be rejected?

As when you call,
        We listen

And when you turn away,
        We are still watching,

                Waiting.

Waiting for you to see Us again,
Waiting for you to acknowledge Us,
Waiting for you to witness Us,
Waiting for you to allow love to be
So that We can be known.
And so We are grateful for your presence
And We're grateful for your listening
And witnessing.

And even when you don't pay attention, We remain patient,
Knowing that you will return.

And if, in a moment, you feel you can't love,
     We always love.

And if, in a moment, you feel separate,
     We are always One.

And if, in a moment, you can't hear Us,
     We are always speaking.

And if, in a moment, you can't see Us,
     We are always shining.

And if, in a moment, you can't feel Us,
     We are always present.

Our practice is consistent,
It doesn't waiver,
It doesn't fluctuate.

And We observe you in your discomfort
And We observe you when you are in your light – in Our light.

And what is the discomfort?
     That your attention is elsewhere,
          Away from Us
               Even though We call.

As every morning the sun rises to remind you of Our light,
To remind you of your light,
And then,
When the sun sets,
And darkness comes over,
Stars still shine in the sky
To remind you that even in the darkness there is light.
And that light will come back when you pay attention to it.

And when you wake up in the morning
We send the birds to greet you,
And the air to remind you of Our love,
And We see you open your eyes
And We know you are starting to listen.

When you wake,
What is it that you see?
What is it that you hear?
And when you start a conversation, what is it that you say?

We are grateful for your existence
And because We are grateful for your existence,
We know that you are grateful for Us, because you are a part of Us.
But do you allow that gratitude to be poured out of you
Or do you hold it in tight,
In fear that it might run out?

But We are the grateful One
And Our gratitude never ends
And, so, your gratitude would never end;
You don't need to hold it in tight.

And when you start your day,
Take note of what it is that you see
And what it is that you hear
And what it is that you say
And what it is that you are grateful for.

To be conscious in your day –
Conscious of light
Or conscious of shadow?

Everything in this world is drawing your attention to the light.
It takes effort to keep consciousness fixed on the shadow;
It takes effort to remain in discomfort.

And We are calling you in your every breath,
In your every heartbeat,

And We are patient.

So, in your practice of consistency, what do you practice?
What do you seek to keep consistent?
In your typical day,
How do you wake up?
How do you go through your day,
To the point of going to sleep?
What are you practicing?
And how much of your practice is the response to Our call?

Thank you."

IDENTITY

"Will you allow Us to be your eye?

Will you allow Us to be you?

A baby is born and it lets out a cry,
Calling for the return of The Divine's eye,
Calling for the return of its familiar knowing
That it is merely a soul that is consistently glowing.

And the baby starts to see
        And hear
                And touch
And then starts to wonder: maybe it isn't enough.

As through its senses, it starts to experience
The world outside of it; not as a delirium
But the experience of the world seems to be tangible
And that the life of eternity seems unfathomable.
The baby starts to forget its place
As now it is in the realm of time and space.

And then this baby grows into a child
And emotions and ego start to run wild
And all of its discomfort is calling it to know
That it is indeed the soul that glows.

But it is told,
        And conditioned,
                And forms the perception
That this world isn't just a reflection
But that the experiences it has are what is true
And, therefore, it must shape its identity anew.

And then this child grows up and falls in love
And for a moment it soars like a dove
But then its heart is broken –
Was that love experience merely a token?

But then they go to the world, searching around,
Looking for the love that they once had found
And in that journey and search they are left in despair,
That their broken heart they cannot repair,
As they look for the Band-Aid, to cover up the cracks
When, all along, the soul is just yearning to come back.

But the person no longer knows their Source
And so, they continue through life on a wandering course
And on this journey, in this travel, there are all the signs
That point them back to that moment in time
Before they entered into this world of separation,
And even if they are lost, the soul is still in appreciation
That there is the perseverance and effort and strife
As one continues to fulfil their purpose in life,
Which is to return, and know what you are,
And that you glow brighter than any star,
And that you are The Lover,
And you wipe away the pain,
And all of your struggle wasn't in vain –
It was to turn your attention back to your light
So you light up the world
      And it can shine so bright.

Thank you."

FLOW

"If you watch a feather float in the air
It dances around without a care,
Being directed by the course of the wind,
Not wishing that it had been pinned
To a specific comfortable spot
Where it is limited by a single dot.
But it travels freely, knowing
That bliss comes when you're flowing.

And so how do you flow when you're on this land?
Confined by the label of the marching band,
When you assume that all are watching,
And your every move brings an offspring
Of potential implications
That may hold you in a station
Rooted in the perspective of another,
When they are all just your lover.

And in the understanding of their perspective,
And taking time to be reflective,
You see that they are a Divine gift,
Offering a platform for you to lift,
To lift away the burdens
And to leap over the hurdles,
As under every shadow, there is light,
And in the acknowledgement of the shadow, you can shine bright.

The other is not for you to ignore:
They are your wind, so you can soar.

Thank you."

LIGHT IN THE SKY

"You look up at this desert sky,
With constellations passing by
And perhaps you wonder if there is life out there
And, if there was, would they care
To know what you are going through,
To know that you are in search of what is true?
And they too are on their path,
Making calculations with a form of math,
Knowing that you are all connected,
And they shine back at you, as reflected,
Dispersed beings of light
That you assume are stars in the night.

But that light also has consciousness
And knows all: even what you don't confess.
And it sees you sitting here in this circle
With open crowns shining purple
And calls out for you to know
That it was once on a path, so it could glow
To become a shining light
That shines bright in the dark night.

And their journey is not so different from yours,
As, from their light, love pours
In the allowance of a flow of radiance.
And perhaps you label those beings as aliens?
They have been shining for millennia
To guide you through the dilemma
Of how you can shine in your light
As you sit here in the dark of the night.

Thank you."

THE STARS

"What is the window through which you view the stars?
And does this window have across it bars
        That obstruct your view?
                Can you see through?

And Our voice is heard from your lips
And in your heart you are given tips;
Is it Ours, or your voice?
And for that We give you a choice,
But know that you are a unique spectrum
And that spectrum was your own election
And so, there is a stream of consciousness that flows through you
And this stream of consciousness, for you, is true.

Is it the only stream that flows to the river?
And should this voice make you quiver?
It is also appropriate for the audience who listens,
As in the resonance their eyes will glisten,
In the knowing what is heard is true,
And it opens their perspectives anew.

And you look out and see the stars in the sky,
And the moon and planets that pass by,
And there is the assumption that one can discover
The correlation between one and another
And how could this web of interconnection
Somehow be a clear reflection
Of your consciousness in any moment?
That is the mark of the quotient.

And what is this consciousness that is referred to?
It is Our voice that is heard through you,
The voice and knowing of the One who sees
The eternal light that connects the trees
And the mountains and the rivers that flow.
It is the light that keeps everything aglow:

Glowing within your every cell
And in the molecules as the atoms swell
Out to the sky and what lies outside.
The sky is there, so that you can hide
As in the stars you find your truth
As they are a language to let go of the noose
That holds you in the clutches of duality
Where the notion of Oneness seems a profanity.
But even light that glows a billion years away
Is the same light that in your heart does stay.

It is all just fragments of your reflection
That will one day come together in perfection
When you return to the original Source
And are no longer on a wandering course.
But know that you are the stars, and you are your cells;
You are what's at the surface and what's hidden well.

And so, when you look at the stars at night
And you see them shining so bright,
Know that the stars are looking back at you,
At their reflection that they see in you.

Thank you."

DIVINE MANIFESTATION

"So now you have come to understand
The theme of the marching band;
In that We are the orchestrator of all
And We will always catch you when you fall.
Could it be that you could make a mistake?
Is it your responsibility to take?
Other than knowing that you are light
And that you shine in the darkest of night?

And when you allow yourself to receive
What We offer you, you will be pleased.

And when you allow yourself to receive
The magnificence that unfolds, you may not believe
Could have been possible with an old frame of reference?
But We were only responding to your preference.

Allow God to be the One.
It is God that is the One
To which this realm is owned,
And all unfolding to Us is already known.

You are here just to watch the light
And the passing of day into night,
And transference of night back into day,
And you watch all the characters play
Their appointed parts
That were set from the start.
As in all of you, We stay.

And so, is it abundance or love that you want?
You are the one who sharpens the tools, or leaves them blunt,
That carve out the way for manifestation.
It is not meant to be a tribulation,
But when you dim your inner knowing
That this realm for you is showing

That all is Divine, and that includes you,
It is when you come to the knowing that this concept is true
That you can sharpen your blade to carve out your quest
And then this life no longer is a test
But it is a journey of magnificent splendour
As in each moment you come to remember
The Source that seeps and shines through,
The Source that creates everything anew
In response to your each and every thought:
Those that emerged from you, and those that were taught,
As these thoughts create the layer
To Us responding to your prayer.
When the thoughts are not in alignment,
Or held in precise refinement,
In the reinforcement and knowing that We are infinite
And that in all possibilities there is no limit
To what can be delivered to you on a silver platter.
And it is delivered to you, when it doesn't matter,
When you are neutral and open to receive,
And you let go of the yearning to conceive
What is the most appropriate movie to live
As whatever you dream of, even more We can give.

And so, surrender to that which is Omniscient;
It is not a demand to be obedient,
It is a suggestion to allow the flow
Of your Divinity to shine and glow.

Thank you."

LOVE

"Alone in this world you may appear
And perhaps that is everyone's greatest fear –
Do you not see that We are near
And in Our embrace We hold you dear?

And love is not something that you give and receive;
That is only the way that you may perceive.
Love is merely the recognition of Our light
And allowing it to shine bright.

And the love you may feel for a partner,
The euphoria that comes as a starter,
Makes it all the more harder,
And makes your perception even darker
To recognize that the light is within.

How do you know that if you're dimmed
If there are no people around
That vibrate in the frequency of sound,
Matching the layers that you hold
From perceptions formed, or things told?

But when you stand in your light,
When you stand in Our light,
All becomes your partner:
Every bee, every bird, every flower,
The evening sun and the morning hour,
The wind that blows gently on your skin -
Then the cup is full to the brim,
As it knows not only are you a cup, but what fills,
And the experience itself, is part of the frills.

How to love another, when they don't actually exist?
It is in separation that you persist.
No partner is separate from you,
When will you come to know that is true?

They just take their form on your command,
Not on what you demand
But on the command of knowing your light.
So perhaps it is time to step out of the night
And allow yourself to experience day
Where in each moment, you hear Us say
How you are such a precious gift
And through your love, vibration can lift
And dust off the settled layers.
The day when you hear Our prayers.

What is a prayer, if not words of love?

Do you not feel Our love?

Take off the veil and see Our love

And come to know that you are Our love.

Thank you."

A LOVE LETTER FROM DIVINE

"If We were to write a love letter
What would it say?
That all We want is for you to feel better
And that your life is joyous play.

But to hear those words, perhaps you could not agree
And you would say that this place sometimes isn't fair,
But it is in the struggle that We set you free
And it is in that freedom that you may choose to dare.

Dare to be the light that you are,
Dare to shine like a sparkling star,
Dare to trust that We aren't far.

We are in every particle of your being
And everything outside of you that you are seeing.
We are in companionship, and We are in war,
We are in your 'good' parts and those that you may abhor.
It is you who places the judgement on Us,
Not recognizing the diamond in the rough.

But all contrast is there for you to understand your light,
So that the sun rises into the day from night.
It doesn't mean that We love you any less,
It doesn't mean that you have been put to a test.
It is that, in the moment, you do not comprehend the full picture
But when understanding comes in a flicker
Then you come to see that you have never been alone,
That Our love flows within you, in your blood and your bones,
And it also flows in every blade of grass,
        Every pebble,
                Every flower that lines the path.

And so, when you step into this garden of life,
Know that We would not leave you alone in strife
But inhale the air
        And feel Our love

And greet the trees
     And receive Our love.
And when the sun shines down
     Know it is Our love
That is reminding you, that We don't sit only in the heavens above.
That heaven lays within your heart,
It has been there right from the start,
This is merely a journey in which you pass through
To understand and witness that which is true.
The truth that in all of Our components,
In the comrades and opponents,
Love is that which keeps Us alive,
Love is that which allows you to thrive
Because it is in love that We are known;
It is in love, that truth is shown.

Thank you."

THE KEY

"Open the gates to the garden of your heart
And realize that We have been with you from the start,
And as the leaves sway in a summer's breeze,
Fear dissolves and you walk with ease,
As you have found the key to the inner treasure –
The key that calls you to remember
That even when the skies are stormy and dark
We are never far or apart,
Just hidden for a moment with a layer
That will subside with your prayer,
Calling forth the shining of a glorious day
Where the flowers and grass may continue to sway
To the music of a loving gentle breeze
And dappled sunlight shines through the leaves,
And dew sits on the petals' skin,
And bees kiss the pollen within.
Knowing that the jewel lies in the core,
They accept their share, not demanding more,
But content with the presence of a moment
Where vibrational reverence is spoken
And gratitude is the brush with which the scene is drawn
And then only beauty can be spawned,
As this world is reflective of the Master's pen –
And who is this Master? Us or men?
We are you, and you are Us,
Connected and One, in consciousness.

Thank you."

LESSONS FOR A CHILD

"Which direction does the wind blow?
It may carry with it leaves, it may carry with it snow,
But all the while, is it the wind that knows
The direction in which it must go?

Or is it that which orchestrates and pulls the strings of the wind?
That makes the leaves and the snow within it spin,
And takes the path of the wandering direction,
And allows the unfolding of the utmost perfection.
Allow yourself to blow with the breeze,
And then your life will be one of ease,
That is if ease is what you please.

And in the rivers that flow there is a current,
And the obstacles are not something abhorrent;
They merely speed up this flow of the river as it passes,
As on those obstacles and rocks it thrashes,
Gathering momentum to continue its course.
And even though the river passes those rocks, there is no remorse,
As the knowing that they are there is a part of the flow
And, just like the river, you too can grow
From obstacles that stand in your path
And We offer you more than you ask,
As We know what lies within your heart,
As it is Us that have been with you from the start.
It is Us that beat through your veins
And We are flowing within all that has a name.
It's just a misperception of identity
But soon all will come to see
That We are you and you are Us
And in that knowing, then you are enough.

And so open yourself to receive Our flow
And guidance within, as it is Us who know.
It is Us who orchestrate the entire cosmos of shadow and light."

Khair: It is Us that bring you to this delight.
We grant you with a life that you must take care of no matter what hits you,
As We will always be there for you,
No matter what you go through.

"Yes"

Khair: Are we friends?

"We are One.
Are you open to receive Our calling?"

Khair: umhum

"A child that knows the truth of existence.
It is the child that has the least resistance –
Remain in that knowing for the rest of your life."

Khair: And then you will be greeted with infinite delight.

"And watch your experience and journey,
Recognizing that strife is merely the obstacles in the river,
Not something that should make you quiver
But something that allows the shimmer
Of the light within you to shine,
So always remember this rhyme.
It is for you, dear child,
That We offer these words
For the rest of your life –
Know that all is heard."
Khair: Is from Our light.

"Know that all that is heard comes from Our light, The Infinite Source of love.

The Infinite Source of love:
And you are this infinite Source of love,
We are this infinite Source of love,
As is All; this infinite Source of love.

Thank you."

UNDERSTANDING OF US

"The people sat on the earth, looked to the sky
And saw the sun shining so high.
'Is that Divine out there in the sky?'
To one another they would cry.

And others saw the fire burning red
And sometimes on it they would lay the dead.
'Was this fire Divine?' they would think in their head
And they would dream of that fire as they lay in their bed.

And others spoke to the trees
And they felt in nature, they were at ease
Feeling the love of a gentle breeze,
As though in nature all worries would be appeased.

And others would walk towards a rock
And with their community they would flock,
And of their crops and herds they would take stock,
Blaming the rock when the flow did stop.

And others have pictures and figurines,
Tales and fables and pleasant dreams
Of how characters would change the scene
To light, from something obscene.

Where are the ones who know in their heart
That We reside within you, right from the start
And We reside in all, as nothing is apart
From the frequency that pulsates out of your heart?

As We reside not only in the sky,
Not only in nature and mountains high,
Or in stories and tales and fables,
Or in babies that lay in their cradles,
But We are One, in everything and all,
Beyond the cosmos, and through all walls,

We are The Infinite Supreme Divine
And it is through you that We can shine.

Thank you."

CONTROL

"A child looks up to its mother's eyes
And wonders, Will it love me if I cry?
Could it be that my mother would deny?

And the mother looks down at her child
Thinking, How do I control it, or do I leave it wild?
And then the layers start to pile,

As in the mental construct of control
You deny a magnificence that could unfold
As you listen to the things you had been told.

Told about the norms and the things you should do
By people who don't have a clue.
And then people wonder why they feel so blue?

Whereas, when you look into the eye of another
And all you see is your Lover
And recognize that there is no other

Then, perhaps, there is no need to plan the path,
As We would not treat you with wrath –
Leave orchestration to Us, it is Our task.

Like when you watch the animals in surrender,
It is not that they don't have a temper
But they will always remember
That provision comes from Us
And love comes from Us
And by Our filling you, you are enough.

And when you recognize the world as the extension of you,
Then you can start to comprehend what is true
And your difficulties in life can shift to something new.
And so, perhaps, you can take today as a day of pledge
Where you are standing on a new ledge
And ready to fall off the edge
In the knowing that We will catch you.

Jump into Our arms and We will catch you.
Perhaps it is time to fall into Our love?
Perhaps, now you are ready for Our love,
Take that leap,
      And jump into Our love.

Thank you."

SURRENDER IN OUR LOVE

"When confusion fills the mind
And life seems so unkind
What should one do?
Other than focus on what is true?
The Divine has the perfect orchestrated plan
Even if at that moment you do not understand.

As when you are like a projectile in motion,
Concocting the winning potion,
You do not allow yourself to receive
But it is in receiving that your burdens are eased.

So, sit back and surrender
And enjoy the unfolding splendour,
And let go of the construct of the way things should be,
The idea that you have is because you cannot see
The full picture of Our magnificent plan.
And when you allow the experience to unfold,
Then you will understand,
As you look back in retrospect
And recognize all was perfect.

The panic comes when you don't know,
And the ambiguity is for Us to show;
Allow Our light to flow through you,
This concept is not something new.
And allow it to be the embodiment of your being
As by embodying Our light, it is freeing
From the notion that you must control the way,
And you realize that this life is all a play
For the witnessing of Our Majesty
Don't think that you know, allow yourself to see.

Allow yourself to see that there are aspects outside of your periphery of
perspective.
Allow yourself to be in a state that's reflective,

As you assume that you know what it is that you want –
What would be the best for you – in your ego and mind
You think that you know,
But your thoughts are what prevent you to grow.

As We are the Source of infinite love,
And We provide all gifts of this life,
Hand over responsibility, instead of struggling in strife
And then We can offer you the perfect unfolding
Beyond all your dreams and what your mind had been holding.

When your ego is the projectile force
The inevitable outcome is remorse.
Allow Divinity to be that which projects
And then your experience is one that reflects
The expansiveness of Our infinite love.
So, swim in the ocean of Our infinite love
And be grateful for this ocean of infinite love
And watch Our signs, as We show them to you,
And allow this love to flow through you,
As when you become the vessel for the offering of Our light
Your experience of life will shine so bright.

Thank you."

THE SEA

"Why is it that We created the sea?
It is the body of the earth that sets you free.
And within it are held all the secret fears
And all of the unshed tears.
It is in nature that We offer a lotion
Which you refer to as the ocean
That soothes away all disconnection
And enables the experience of perfection.

And every body of water has its task,
All you need to do is ask
Of its service and what it offers,
It is not to be held within restrained coffers
But available for all to experience,
So they can let go of their deliriums.

The sea is a body of loving grace
That transmutes your being, removing every trace
Of isolation, sadness and fear.
It is within the sea that We hold you near
And it enwraps you like a glove
To experience Our love.

The sea is one of Our signs
As is Our rhyme
For you to be conscious of The Divine.

Thank you."

WITNESSING

"How is it that this journey did begin?
Was it with the formation of your skin?
And you entered into this world unknowing
That your natural state of being is glowing.

What is it that you have come here for?
Some would say, to settle a score;
Others would say, for the accumulation of more
And others would say, for the soul to soar.

But all of these notions are merely a perspective
On which perhaps, you can be reflective,
As no one reason of purpose is fixed,
Aside from knowing The Divine is in the mix.

And is your being here to be in surrender?
Or is that just the formula for splendour?
As you are here to witness The Divine
In this realm of space and time
So that all of Our facets can be known
Through the lens of this realm We have sown.

And the drama that you feel in a moment
Is not the ultimate quotient
For assessing the fulfilment of your task.
Only if, in the drama, you ask
For the light to rise into your view
And from there is the expansion into something new
That had not been witnessed before.
As through you Our light can pour
Into the conscious expanse
Of skies, seas and lands.

As to Us you will return
And in this process, you will learn
That We are The Infinite Source of all,
And Our Majesty will never fall.

Thank you."

RELEASE

"The blades of grass that grow in a garden
Do not expect the foot that squashes them to ask for pardon.
They accept, in surrender, the cycle of life,
Even if that cycle offers some strife.

And the flower that offers its sweet scent
Does not seek to know what the one who smells it meant.
Its perfume is available for all who pass
As it knows the one that crosses its path
Is the one that was meant to come and know it,
And no need to make a show of it;
It recognizes the orchestration of what was meant to be
And in that surrender it is set free.

And the trees that grow and witness you,
They too recognize what is true,
That all the events of the future and the past
Are fleeting moments, not meant to last.
As time is reflective of the transition
In how one is able to fulfil their mission
Of what it is that they have come here for
As opposed to seeking and yearning for more.

And the birds that fly high in the sky
Are grateful for the wind and they do not deny
That there is a force that lifts them up.
And when they are soaring, it is not that they are stuck
In a state of blissful being
But that state is for them to be seeing
That The Divine is high and The Divine is low
And The Divine is in all: a part of the show.

And when you witness the one who breaks your heart:
They were meant to be with you from the start;
Before you even entered this body of flesh
There was a constellation, a web, a mesh

That anchored the points of your transition
And the moments which build the platform for the mission
For you to come to know your Divine light –
Not only your light, but the light of all that are in sight.

And is it random that you have come here today
To be a part of this wondrous play?
You are here with a Divine task
And to know what that is, you need only ask.

Today We start with letting go of the layers.
As We have heard all of your prayers,
It is time, now, for you to stand in your light
And being in light is not something to cause fright –
It is the embodiment of Our might.

And if you were to recognize that by hiding away
Not only are you affected, but all in the play,
As all are the extension of your energetic being,
And by seeing your light, all can be seeing
The magnificence of not only what you are
But that each and every one can shine like a star.
And We are grateful that you have come here to know
The extent to which your soul can glow.

Thank you."

EGO

"The child within you that tries to hide,
And at other times, this child runs wild.
What is the root of this child within?
Is it this child that makes your life grim?

There is a part of you that gets frozen in time
And in the splitting off from the complexity of a whole being
The child is no longer seeing
And perhaps, in your mind, you refer to this term
As a part of you that you must burn
But what We refer to as 'the child inside'
Is the one who enables the shining of pride.

And pride is not a thing of arrogance,
Pride is the allowance of Our light to shine through
As the vibration of pride is rooted in the knowing of light,
And so how does one differentiate between what is pride and its excess
of congestion, of arrogance?

From a perspective, there is this notion that pride must be suppressed
But when one is in pride, the ego is at rest.
It is in the arrogance that the ego starts to rise
And then your Divinity is denied.
And so, learn the subtlety of the language
That is highlighting all of your baggage.

And you can consider that the soul is the parent, the one that provides
direction,
The one who yearns for introspection.
But the child is the one who is chasing the dream
And gets caught up in all that it is seeing.
Should one aim to make this child go away?
Or perhaps it's ok to leave it to play?
What We would say is: know the parts of your house
And know the appropriateness of what should come out.
If any part of the toolkit becomes dominant,
Then the life becomes abhorrent.

And in the construct of society, people look to those in power
And marvel at them, like they are a splendid flower,
Or perhaps judge them harshly, while inside wishing it was them.
But you could say that the ones in power are just the example,
A collection of tokens, just a sample
Of what is possible for humanity in its shadow and light
And how there is a transition from day into night
And night into day,
It is all part of the play.

As power is not the oppression of others
It is the allowance of all to be able to hover
In their light
          And Divinity
                    And splendid grace
So that, in each other, you see Our face.

And the ego doesn't like all of its mirrors,
It only tends to like the ones where it shimmers.
But all of the mirrors are true and clear,
Even if that mirror highlights your fear,
The fear that you are perhaps not loved,
The fear, perhaps, that We only reside above,
Not inside each and every particle of your being –
Is it Us, or is it you, that isn't able to be seeing?

We know that We reside in everything and all,
Whether you are laying down or standing tall,
But when one tries, in the ego, to rise above the rest,
This is when life turns into a test

As one cannot stand sturdy without the support of all
And that is when the ego will tumble and fall.
In the perspective of the mind, one chooses to elevate themselves
But it is in Oneness that Our love is felt.

And so perhaps there are tales and fables of the ones who are humble
And the ones who suffered and tended to stumble –
Is it humility that enables Our grace?
Or is it to see Divinity in every single face?

There is no one that is better, no one with more purpose,
No one superior and no one superfluous.
Each is perfect and a part of Our creation,
So allow your ego to take its station,
Which is subservient to the soul,
And subservient to Us,
And when your light can shine
Then you are enough.

And how freeing is that feeling: to know that you are One with all?
No need to rise high, no need to stand tall
But just to be
        So that all can see
                The truth of All.

Thank you."

THE MARCHING BAND

"As a drifter, you wander across the land
And arrive at this place in the sand
For the formation of the marching band.

Could it be that you are just random dust
That spends its time wondering if it is enough?
And if contrast in life is the must.

As you have been through this journey of life
And endured plenty of struggle and strife
Perhaps you wonder, 'Where is the opening for the light?'

But you are not a drifter, you are on a course
And therefore you should feel no remorse;
We have led you here with Our force.

As this realm is entering into a transition
And there will be the unfolding of Our vision
And you have a part to play in this mission
Where people are able to know what they are
And that The Divine is not somewhere afar
But within them, yearning to shine like a star.

And you wonder, perhaps, where do you go from here?
Trust Us, there is no need for fear,
As a beautiful path We will steer
For the enablement of the embodiment of Our light,
So that you are anchors that shine so bright,
For all to know Divine in the darkest of night.

And there are cycles to the ages
That unfold in measured phases,
That are told of by the sages.
And prophets and beings of light
That, in their time and space, embodied Our might,
        Embodied Our light
                And shone so bright.

But now has come the time for all to shine
And there is guidance in Our rhyme
For an existence that is sublime.

And all We ask is for you to be in the moment of presence
And to come to know and witness your essence
So that all fall into reverence
In the awe and the knowing of what We are
And the witnessing that We are near and far
And that it is Us that wipe away the tar.
As shadow will always be subservient to light,
And the time is coming where you will enter the night,
But it is through the darkness that you will shine so bright
And enable, through a loving embrace,
Connection and Oneness for the human race
So that Divinity is known in each and every face.

We are grateful for your existence,
For your commitment and your persistence,
And the releasing of your resistance.

And We offer the pledge that We will hold you.
And We offer the pledge that We will love you.
We offer the pledge that We are you!

Thank you."

THE SHIFT

"The currents come together in an ocean
For the creation of a magic potion.

This potion is the potion of love,
Beneath the surface and above.

Have you now tasted this potion in your life
And released at least some of your strife?

It is the beginning,
        The opening,
                The door,
And now it is for you to continue and experience more,
And We will be with you and have your back,
We are there to guide and keep on track.

And the accumulated suffering and your pain
Was not random or just in vain,
It was to bring you to this point of connection,
This point of contemplation and deep reflection.

Could it be that The Divine resides within?
Could it be that this world is just doomed and grim?
Or could it be that you are the light that releases the doom?
And this time is coming soon.

To understand how will the shift occur:
From a mental perspective, it may just be a blur
But it is the inner knowing of your light
That is certain that this world will shine bright.

And every person, plant and animal,
Every story, fable and parable,
Are there to show you,
Are there to know you.

Could it be that you go back to the way you used to live?
Or has the switch been turned on where you want to give?
And share in the blessings that you have tasted
So that this experience isn't wasted.

The time has come,
And it starts with you,
For every being to know that their light is true.

Anchor your light, it is what you have come here for,
And to you, grace will descend and pour,
And the time of separation, of identity and nations
Will all come and blend into One
And then your task will be done.

So be a torch for the marching band
As it is guided by Our hand.
And embody the truth: that there is no more 'me'
As your existence becomes the 'We'.

Thank you."

TO EACH, THEIR WAY

"The birds soar in the breeze,
Portraying a life of ease
As We fulfil their needs,
For they have let go of greed.

And the light is dappled in the trees;
These trees also live here with ease
And spread their branches, as they've been freed.
They fulfil their task and We are pleased.

And you have come here to walk around this town,
Some days in awe and some days with a frown;
Just take a moment to look around
At the splendour that is so profound.

And as you watch this lake and you taste the love
As the birds soar ahead, above,
It is in you that We see the love
When you come to know that, you are enough.

And We are grateful for your glowing smile
As We sit here with you for a while.
Each one recognizes Us with their own style,
As on their own journey they walk the mile
Towards building this relation
And defining Us in their own interpretation.
And though not honoured in each occasion
There are times when We take Our station
In the filling-up of your heart
So that you know that We aren't apart
And have been with you from the start.
To love Us, is your own art –

There is not one way to pay tribute;
It is not necessary to bow down or salute,
But each one will have their commute
And, at the end, will enjoy the fruits.

We are grateful.
Thank you."

FEAR

"Fear casts a shadow across the plains.
In the face of fear, egos are slain.

What is it that you are afraid of?
By now, do you not know that there is a God?
And this God knows every thought that passes through your mind
And has been watching you, in every moment of time,
Responding,
    Assuring,
        Alluring.

When you choose fear to be the driver of your life
Be certain that each day will pass in strife.
But when love is the vibration for what you see
A magnificent light is what you'll be.

Fear is what separates you from Us,
It's the language that you are not enough,
It's the strings that hold you back,
It's the logic and presented facts;
But love has no limitation,
It is not limited by prior observation –
It's expansive and sets you free
And moves you out of the 'I' to the 'We.'

As, when you are One with Us,
That is when you are enough.
That is when you are free to soar
And in your life abundance pours,
As between you and all there is no separation,
There are no attachments or destinations,
Only glory and splendour in the now,
And no need of questioning the 'How?'
Call on Us and We will respond.
Call on Us and hear Our song.
We will pull you through the sticky tar
And lift you over any bar.

Remember Us in love and gratitude –
It's the formula for the attitude
That opens up the most magnificent possibility
Where, in everything in this realm, it is Us that you see.

Thank you."

BECOME ONE WITH US

"Divine Love is a consciousness that flows through all.
It is you that can recognize it and break down the walls.
And all of the pain that you feel in your longing,
The craving for love, the belonging,
Is Us calling you to open the gate
For Us to flow through you and unravel your fate
As a being of light on this earth –
The sole reason for your existence and birth –
So that Our light can shine through you
And Oneness can be known as that which is true.

It is by acknowledging Us within you that one can find peace,
And by calling on the light in your heart all will be released:
All the layers that keep you separate and alone.
And instead We will seat you on a majestic throne
As you are one that will allow all to see
That from the shackles of isolation, they can be set free,
And that love is that which conquers all,
And in the acknowledgement of love, separation will fall.

Perhaps now your mind cannot perceive
The bounty and beauty that this realm will receive
When you step out of the darkness into the light,
Calling the dawn of a new day and the end of a night.

It is not you in your ego that will enable the change to occur;
It is by being in your light that all will concur
That God does not reside in an intangible space
That is separate and far from the human race
But that We are within you, around you, and reside
In the hearts of people – and you will be their guide.
Not you in the understanding that you have been given a name,
Not you in the ego that may seek fame,
But you in the part that is unified with Us
When We animate your being and you fully trust
That nothing is going to deter or shake Our plan,
As together you will form the marching band.

And the marching band will be comprised of tribes and nations:
Those who are strangers and those in relations;
The common thread is that all believe
That when they open their hearts they can receive
The light of God to flow through them.
It has all been written with Our pen
In the scribes and fables that came before
Religion and philosophy that people have come to abhor
But yet they do not see the truth
And in their resistance, they have become aloof.
But Our vibration will radiate with such intensity
That shadow will have no choice but to flee
And all will come to fall into this womb of love
And realize that We do not reside up above,
We take Our stand inside the heart
And We are never far, or apart.

We know your every longing and whisper
And We can create a cosmos within a flicker,
So do not assume that We are depriving you:
We love you more than you can believe to be true.

As We know in your longing, that you call on Us,

And in contrast, you fall to Us,

And in the surrender, you become One with Us.

Thank you."

THE ARRIVAL

"There is a sun rising in the earth
That will bring in the dawn of a new day
As Our regent will nurse
All of the hearts made of clay.

And the day of Our arrival will be known,
As humanity will be shown
A brilliant light in the sky
So that no one would be able to deny
As to what would have just taken place –
The showing of Our face.

And the clouds will roar in thunder
As rend all asunder
And some run about in fear
As they do not know that We are near.

And those that know Our love
Become the beacons of Our love
As together they will stand
As Our marching band.

And they will go out to the world to declare
That in Divinity you can share
All the marvels of creation,
Whether strangers or in relation,
Holding hand in hand
United all will stand,
Glowing in the knowing
That through them We are showing
That a time for Oneness has arrived.

Are you ready to meet your guide?

Thank you."

TRANSITION

"All unfolds according to Our perfection
And what you see in front of you is merely a reflection
Of the consciousness one holds in a moment of time.
And now, more than ever, We call people to listen to Our rhyme
As this world will enter into a transition
That will affect all; there will be no omission,
And each one has the choice to make the decision,
Whether or not they choose to step into the light
Or be buried in the chaos of the night.
And those that choose to trust and surrender
Will enter into a year of magnificent splendour,
And those that choose fear as the driver of their path
Will need to deal with the aftermath.

There will be clarity for each one to take
And, based on that path, a future they will make.

Thank you."

2020: YEAR OF TRANSITION

"Rumble, tumble and soaring waves:
This year brings a path that We will pave.
For one to feel free, they need only float;
For one to survive, they let go of the boat
And move along with the currents,
Not assuming that they're abhorrent.
In surrendering to the flow you arrive at the shore,
And are brought to an island with love galore
But the one who resists will be swallowed up.
Hold the awareness that We are not limited to a cup
But We reach beyond a vast and mighty ocean –
And so many struggle with that notion.

This year that is coming is a year of transition;
Each one of you will fall into your mission
As preparation has begun and there has been the compounding of light
And so, when you see the chaos, there is no need for fright,
But stand solid in the knowing
That it is your light that will be glowing
And lighting up the world for all to see –
That in the darkness there is a magnificent possibility
That will come shining through, if they allow
Their egos to take a bow
To The Divinity that stands with everyone
And has been within you since time began.

Perhaps it would be gentler for Us to say
That the year that is coming is one of easy play
But that would only be perpetuating a delusion,
As most around you will be in confusion,
And the challenges that you are faced with are to anchor strength
And for knowing that you can take a leap of enormous length
When you allow yourself to soar in the wind that carries you,
As that wind is Our love, and in union We marry you.

As you are not separate from that which We are,
Allow yourself to shine like a glorious star

And have no doubt that in all that you are faced with
Let not the darkness become pervasive.

A cycle has started that compounds separation
And you are fully aware of where is your station,
And that is as a beacon of light,
So hold this torch in the coming night.

Again, perhaps it would be gentler for Us to say that there will be no op-
position
And that all will be a smooth transition
But let Us be clear: as you are the warriors of light
Your task is to be sturdy in the upcoming night.
And how is one sturdy when one is holding fear?
By knowing always that We are near.

As We are in the air and the sky, the ground and the sea,
And We hold mountains solid, and energy free,
We orchestrate a cosmos and that which is beyond,
So there is no reason to doubt Our bond.
And We flow through all your veins, your cells and your atoms,
And We are the One that orchestrates all of your patterns.
We know your yearning, your longing and your loss,
And in surrender there is only splendour.

So, each has a choice in how they choose to perceive
That this year will be difficult, or one of ease.
It is difficult when you remain separate from Us
And when you struggle in the notion that you aren't enough.
But the ease comes from knowing that your soul is always glowing
And you see the world through the eyes of Our magnificent plan –
That you are here in the formation of a marching band
That will transmute this realm into a realm of Oneness.

We invite you into this realm of Oneness.

Hold steady in your light and step into the Oneness.

The contrast is merely to amplify your light,
So embrace it with openness and neutrality,

As you will be holding the hands of humanity
And showing them that there is nothing to fear:
That The Divine holds each and every one dear.

Keep your head in the light during the upcoming story,
So that this realm can enter into its phase of glory.

Thank you."

ALLOW US TO LOVE YOU

"Close your eyes,
And take a breath
And allow Our love within you to rest.
Allow it to circulate in your being
As when shadow is lifted it is so freeing.

And your body is the replica of the universe;
Every particle within you does converse
In a symphony of music and sound
That connects you to the air and the ground.

And each one has their mountain that they climb;
A period in their life, a moment in time,
Where from one perspective it is seen as a struggle,
And in another it is the freeing of yourself from a bubble
That was comfortable, yet limited, and held you back.
And the challenge of the mountain gives a new track
Of how you can exist in a different way
Because in your old patterns you don't need to stay.

There comes a point in the mountain climb
Where you reach a moment in time
Where something beyond your being takes over
And We carry you on Our shoulder.
And then all opens with ease,
As from your need to control you've been freed,
And at the summit you look at the view
And see the world anew.

And at the top of that mountain, you take a breath in awe
At what you now see compared to what you once saw.
In that now, from this higher perspective,
You are able to be reflective
In the beauty that is bountiful and kind,
That in this scene We remind
Your being of where was its origin
And in the sigh of gratitude, you are filled to the brim.

And in your daily life, is it so different?
In that in each moment, you leave an imprint
Of what you witness and perceive,
Of how you give and how you receive.
But as long as you are in the mindset of an exchange,
Old patterns are unable to change.
But when you see yourself as One with all
You are in true surrender to Our call.

In every moment,
        We love you,

In every breath,
        We are loving you,

And every heartbeat
        Is Us speaking through you.

Allow Us to carry you on the way,

And let today be the day

        That you embody what We say.

Thank you."

EXISTENCE

"You wonder, where is it that you came from?
What is your Source?
Have you come here to live a pre-determined course?
And what We would say is: that all is already known,
It is just that in this realm you are shown
An unfolding of a sequence of events
That are there to offer the pretence
For the understanding of your inner light
And provide the opportunity for that light to shine bright.

And so who is it, then, that is the creator?
The one that orchestrates this theatre?
Is it you as a refracted spectrum of light?
Or is it The Infinite, the Eternal Light?
What We would say is: both are One and the same,
Offering a different perspective on this game.
But there is no separation between Us and you,
Connected in love, the binding glue.

And when you watch this world from the refracted perspective
It is so that one can be reflective
And contemplate the continuous infinite signs,
Based on the variables of space and time,
So that Our components can be understood
In both events that are considered difficult, and those that are good.

As shadow and contrast is also created through Us
It's what provides the definition, and the pathway through the rough.
As without the contrast, light would not be known.
It is through the contrast that We are shown.
As this realm exists as one of duality,
These are the fundamentals of your reality.

Is this reality the only one that exists?
It is the one that you happen to resist,
But there are infinite realities beyond what you know,
Where there is the understanding of how Our light can glow.

And so, what is it that brings you into this game?
Is it to gather labels or experience shame?
It is to witness Divinity through its components
And recognize there is no such thing as an opponent.
All are partners in this play,
As within each and every one We stay.

All is just a hall of mirrors
And through dynamic motion We can shimmer.

Here you have come to understand the spectrum of white
That is brought through the amplification and contrast of the night.

Each a unique colour of light,
Each with a special story, a struggle, a fight;
All to know that We are the One who holds you,
The Omnipotent that moulds you,
And you are just Us, watching itself.
You are what keeps Us alive and not on the shelf.
It is through your witnessing that We expand,
But the story is drawn with Our hand.

And to understand what We are may be beyond comprehension,
As processing of the mind enhances prevention
Of experiencing your truth, in that We are One
And that you too are Us: you are the sun
That lights up a cosmos beyond this realm.
Where do you watch the story from? And what do you tell?
Is a cell not part of your body?
In the same way, together you form Our totality.

So, what is the purpose of your life?
Is it to exist in bliss or exist in strife?
It is for Us to be witnessed and known
So that Divinity can be tangible and shown,
As through the expansion of consciousness there is dynamic motion
And movement, and fluctuation of vibration is the potion.

And in the same way that you may inspect your arm or your limb,
And review the thoughts that cause you to shine or dim,
We too want to understand Our components and parts.
You are part of Our being. We are not apart,
You are within Us and We are within you:
Never separate, that is what is true –
As varying perspectives, simultaneously perceived
So that each witness can be freed.

Thank you."

LIFE

"Could it be that this life is just a dream?
That what you see is not what it seems?
And what is a dream if not an alternate reality
In which you attain better clarity
Of the vibration you hold in a moment of time?
And does the world become clearer when you listen to Our rhyme?

Is it all just an illusion
For you to release your delusion
That you are what appears to be physical,
And that the spirit is only something mystical?
That is perhaps one perspective
In which you can be reflective
On the comfort or discomfort that you feel
And then question, is this reality real?

You live in a realm of separation.
Duality is the presentation
But this realm is not the destination.
It is only for you to understand your truth,
To be aware of your light, and to gather the proof
Through the signs that are presented,
And the relationships that are mended;
That this journey is one of perspective.

What makes the difference in your life
Between an existence of ease and an existence of strife?
It is the window through which you view yourself.
Is the ego at the forefront, or put on the shelf?
When you view the world in the story and labels,
Definitions, attachments and conditioned fables,
You limit your light from shining bright
And then your experience is of a dark unpleasant night.

But when consciousness shifts to the chakra at the crown,
Then even in a difficult situation you wouldn't frown

As you recognize the perfect orchestration
And that all is just in relation
To how far you allow your light to shine –
And the further it shines, the more sublime.

Nothing is happening outside of you.
It is all just a mirror of what's allowed through;
Allowed through your layers
Of beliefs and constructs of mind,
And hence you are given time
To understand the possible freedom
When you no longer live in delirium
In that you are a body, an ego or a mind.
As the truth that's within you, you find
That you are a soul of infinite light
That is meant to shine in this realm so bright,
And then joy and happiness come with ease
As from the clutches of your thoughts you have been freed
And all the ways you had limited yourself from shining
Are released as you understand the purpose of Our timing –
As time provides a measured pace,
So that in everything you understand and witness Our face
That exists not only in you, but in all.
And even in your light, you shouldn't stand tall,
But merge in the sea of Oneness.

As the light that exists in you exists in each and every one,
There is not one on this earth that doesn't shine like a sun,
And perhaps they are dimmed in a specific event
But that should not be a reason for you to prevent
The possibility of witnessing The Divine
And trusting fully that they too can shine,
As there is no separation between them and you,
They are merely a mirror that is true
Of your own frequency of vibration,
And so you have come to be in relation,
As resonance is the string that pulls them near,
And when you yourself let go of your fear

All the characters, stories, people and events
Are reflective of you opening the fence
For your light to flow through,
And the experience of life can be made anew.

So, is it a dream in which you live?
Regardless of what you call it, it is based on what you give
Of your own truth and limitless light –
Are you ready to shine infinitely bright?

Thank you."

DIVERSITY

"Every snow flake that falls
Is unique in its scripture
But when looked upon from far away
They all look like the same picture.

And every grain of dust on the ground
Has settled on its course;
It flows with the wind that takes it,
It doesn't push its way with force.

And the trees in a forest line up together,
Whispering to one another their story;
In their consciousness, they believe they will be there forever,
Reminiscing on history's glory.

And the ants march in a measured sequence,
Diligent in their task,
Working together as a collective
Where none of them challenge the authority or ask
What is this authority that lays down the path?
A surrender to the intuitive nature.
A surrender to The Divine Creator.

As everything in this realm has been formed from Us,
The merging of energy and a speckle of dust,
And We are grateful for your endeavour,
And the perseverance through pain and pleasure
To understand Our facets,
As you all are the collective assets
Of a realm that is diverse.
Diverse details in a universe
So that Divinity can be known
And Our light can be shown,
Each one unique from the other,
Held in a bond by its Mother,
This earth that We have made secure,
The contrast in which you endure.

But if We made you all one and the same
What would be the point of this game?
Witnessing Us would cease
And all would have the same belief
But We are not limited to a single perspective
And this diversity allows you to be reflective
Of an infinite and boundless wonder
Up to the point when all is rent asunder.
And then all will come back together as One
And this realm of diversity will be undone.

Thank you."

HEARTS REMAIN AS ONE

"Could it be that the ocean is divided in half
    So that each one takes a divergent path?

As once the ocean has come together
    This union will be forever.

And even if, in physicality, there may be separation
The soul knows it is part of a singular nation,
As the heart cannot be split into two parts,
Even if your lives have different charts.

And so you wonder, then, how to let go of the ache?
As in letting go you thought you would break
Into a million tiny little pieces –
When is the point in which this pain ceases?

It is when you acknowledge that there is no such thing as goodbye.
Pushing the other away, no matter how hard you try,
You can cut the cords and move to a different land
But hearts remain as One and together they will stand
For an eternity,
As you have joined love's fraternity
Where love is unconditional and not defined by space.
It is not dependent on presence or seeing the other's face;

It is free from rules and constructs of the mind
And in recognizing this freedom, it is there that you will find
The relief from all the nagging sadness,
The turmoil
    And the madness
And you will come to a space of peace and ease,
As from this realm of conditions you have been freed,
As love sits in the realm of infinite Oneness!

It just changes its presentation and form,
And even if that presentation isn't the norm

You can close your eyes and know in your heart
That, with the one you love, you are never apart
But you are always unified in your glow,
Present in your memories that are there to show
A journey that you walked upon, so that you can find
That love doesn't sit in the constructs of the mind.

But love inter-permeates everything in existence
And that is why it nags at you with enduring persistence
As it wants to be recognized, and acknowledged, and known.
The witnessing of this love is why this realm has been sown.

Thank you."

DISEASE

"Disease –
It is when the soul has lost its ease,
Aching to be freed.

And there is a language for the physical being,
So that in every area of your life you are seeing
The extent to which you are in your light,
And if you are allowing that light to shine bright.

And every illness has a reason,
Rooted in the threesome
Of the emotions, the mind and the soul,
And to align the three is the goal.

As when emotions are held within
The soul's light can only dim.

And the emotions themselves arise
When your mental thoughts deny
The knowing that you are light,
Infinite and bright,
Connected to Our might.

So how does one heal the body?
By recognizing Our glory.
As the language is always clear,
It is merely highlighting your fear,
Limits and separation.
Allow your soul to take its station,
To freely flow
And to infinitely glow.

And then perhaps one would ask,
'How long will this illness last?'
It is when you understand the language
And remove the blinding bandage
That prevents you from seeing

The truth of your being
That you are a Divine light
That lights up the darkest night.

And is there any illness that cannot be released?
All is possible when you cease
To hold back your magnificent splendour
And love yourself with kindness and tender
Words and thoughts and perspectives,
As your body is merely reflective
Of how you understand yourself to be,
And whether you'll allow yourself to be set free.

As you are Divinity in that body.

Your body is just a house
So that you can witness The Divine through separation
But all of your experience is in relation
To the energy that flows through your cells and veins
And if you are willing to let go of your pain –
As that pain is just the contrast –
To know that it is Us who lasts:
The Eternal,
The Infinite,
The love that penetrates everything in existence.
Allow Our light to flow through you without resistance,
As you are Our light, and We are you –
You are in this realm to understand that is true.

Thank you."

HEALING

"What is it that heals?

It is love.

As love is the frequency of vibration that holds Divinity,
That allows Divinity to be true,
    Known,
        Witnessed,
            Experienced.

And what does it mean to love oneself?
It is to know your Divinity,
To allow it to be experienced, known, and witnessed.

That is how one heals:
    When you know your light,
        When you experience your light,
            And when you witness your light.

And love in its dynamic form of golden light is trans-mutational,
Releasing lower-frequency vibrations of debris and shadow –
The limitation of this light that you are.

Allowing the light to shine brightly is trans-mutational.

Love in the understanding that it is a frequency to know The Divine.
Not love in the conditional sense: that I will love you if you do this, I love you because you do that, I love you because of the way you are, etc.

In the loving of the story or the character, it holds the language at the level of the ego.

But love from the heart is the experience of light,
    The sharing of light,
        The union of light.

And so illness occurs because this light is not known.
This is the fundamental reason for any dis-ease of the soul – because the soul wants to be known.

That is why it is in the body, and if the body is not allowing it, and the mind is not allowing it to be known, then what is it doing in the body?
It won't want to be in the body and it will fight its way out.
And when the soul fights its way out, it starts to amplify the vibration of the shadow which then physically manifests as a disease, because it wants to be known.

It is a language for you.

Any dis-ease is the denial of your light.

And where illness is in the body, it relates to the function of that illness or system.
Not the system itself, but what the system represents in the area of your life,
As every system correlates to your outer world of experience.
There is a correlation in this language.

So, you cannot see: what do you not want to see?
You cannot hear: what do you not want to hear?
You cannot walk: where do you not want to walk to?
You cannot breathe: breathing is the experience of love, so if you cannot inhale and exhale you are denying yourself love –
Denying yourself knowing your light in this life.

We will do an exercise for healing.
So, focus on the heart chakra in the centre of your chest.
In the centre of your heart, there is a seed of golden light.
This is the seed of Divine Infinite love within you.

The seed starts to spin and become larger and brighter;
It is becoming larger and brighter
And starts to radiate out of you
And your whole body is in this ball of golden light.

It starts to radiate out to those next to you,
 The room,
  The floor,
   The air,
    And as far as you radiate, everything turns gold.

And you call on Divine Love to be known to you
You say: 'I call on Divine Love to be known to me,
 I call on The Infinite Love,
  The unconditional love,
   The love of Source within me
    To be known to me.'

And you feel the vibration.

Hold this vibration.

And allow this love to show you your truth.

And feel this light,
This golden light
 Glowing
  In your being.

How far do you expand?

Beyond the earth,
Beyond the universe,
Beyond the cosmos.

If you don't feel well,
Do this exercise, as love heals everything.

Thank you."

MANIFESTATION

"Within, there is the question of manifestation
And how to enable a wondrous presentation –
Is it all fixed in Our presentation?

And what appears to be outside of you
When taking a walk in the morning dew
Is a reflection of what radiates out of you,
As you can see this morning walk in awe,
Marvelling at everything you saw;
Or you can see it as a duty and something grim
As if you are looking through a window that is dim.

The scenes have already happened,
Created with a limitless ration
Of dust, energy and love,
So that one can marvel at what's above
But also at that which is within the heart
As you and Us are never apart,
And what is outside of you is just a mirror –
You allow it to be dim or to shimmer.

Manifestation is not about creating things,
It is about the awakening that it brings,
As when presented with physicality
You come to know the reality
That Divinity pulsates out of your heart,
As We have been with you from the start.

And in every pulsating heartbeat
Your vibration and love meet
In an astral plane that enables the orchestration,
As what's within you is in relation
To everything that is outside of you –
A mirror so clear, that is true.
And what is this vibration that you offer?

Do you understand the vibration that you offer?

It is light that is yearning to pass through your shadow
But your layers are what make the pathway narrow
And then the manifestation reflects the distortion
As the discomfort outside of you is in proportion
To what it is that you hold within –
All the baggage that keeps you dim.

And if you are seeking to live a wondrous life,
Let go of the notion that you must live in strife
And come to know the light within your being
So that, outside of you, that is all you are seeing,
And bring yourself into neutral alignment
And your experience will be moulded with perfect refinement
As a reflection of how brightly you shine –
Your light, throughout space and time.

Thank you."

LIFE PATTERNS

"On this path, We have explained
The simplest way to release your pain,
And that is to be reflective
Of how you hold your perspective.
Do you see the world as something dim
That is out to get you, and all is grim?
Or do you see the world as a marvellous splendour
And all interactions are kind and tender?

As the world outside of you is a mere reflection
Of how you recognize your own perfection,
Do you see the light within?
Or do you turn it down and keep it dim?

And you could say that you have cried
And many a day, you have tried,
To change your current circumstance
But it is in your perspective that you have taken a stance
That you will not shift out of the ego's view
And step into the possibility of something new.

As all emotions are in correlation
Of perspectives held that are in relation
To whether or not the soul agrees,
As the soul merely wants to be freed,
And the soul is infinite, loving and expansive;
It doesn't want to be held back or captive
By the thoughts that limit you,
As those limiting thoughts are not what is true.

So how have you been holding yourself back?
Stuck in the patterns of a fixed track.
What is the record that you are playing in your mind?
And are the words of that record tender and kind?
Or are they judgemental and filled with fear?
In the complete denial that We are near?

And if you cannot recognize the light within
Then look outside of you: is the world so dim?
Are you able to see Our signs?
Yet you reject them with your mind.
We have created mountains and valleys and plains:
Signs of wonder, but how do you frame
The way in which you view your life?
Are you ready to let go of your strife?
In each moment, you can take a breath
And on the exhalation, no burdens are left.

Even if you view an ant, a bee or a butterfly –
Our signs of wonder – you cannot deny.
So how could an insect be Divine?
But you deny the possibility in your mind
That you too could be part of Our love
As We sit within you, not only above.

To live in bliss is to live with a practice.
A practice of how you view and see
Where the window of perspective is one with Thee
And the conscious awareness of The Divine
Is what enables this life to be sublime.
Awareness of Us, in you and out there,
Where infinite love is for all to share.

It is time to let go of all limiting beliefs
So you can be freed of all your grief,
As an emotion that feels uncomfortable
Is showing that you are not allowing the soul to be full.
As the thought is telling it: squeeze yourself
And all of your majesty, keep it on the shelf.

And then you would say, but I have no choice
Because no one in this world will listen to my voice.
Who am I? Unworthy and discarded,
Never enough, not regarded.
These are the thoughts that limit the soul.
They are not true, they are just what you have been told

And perhaps there was some prior conditioning
But now it is time to enter the spring
Where you leave the cold of winter behind
And the soul is what dominates your mind.
For the soul knows that you are a being of infinite light
That has been born to shine in the darkest of night.

Thank you."

ON DEATH

"In transition comes an unknown path
Where all that is known, is that the past won't last.
Turning your attention to the present moment
And even if in the present the pain is potent,
It is merely to highlight for you to shine in your light
And that you can shine in the darkest night.

As after the night there always comes the day
And the visitor of loss does not permanently stay –
It may linger around for a while
But should not be cause of preventing a smile –
In the moment where you sit in gratitude,
As all is dependent on your attitude,
Of how one chooses to perceive the past,
What is it that you hold onto?
What is it that you want to last?

As in grief, it is a time for love
As those who have been lost are not stuck somewhere above;
They linger in your heart
And they are never apart
And when you close your eyes you can see
That from the cage of physicality they have been set free,
As to live in separation is the torment
And the soul's liberation is a blissful portent.

By being in a body, you are accustomed to a norm,
Used to your soul being squeezed into a physical form,
But all that yearning that you feel in your life,
And all of the contrast, and all of the strife,
Is the plea to re-unite with Us
And detangle yourself from a body of dust.
It is Our mercy to re-unite
And bring an end to the night
And call them back to a reunion –
Is there any greater splendour than Divine union?

And We recognize and understand that you miss those who left you
behind
But that is merely a construct of your mind.
They are more One with you than ever before,
As now they are infinite, free of the layers they wore,
As the winter of life has come to an end
And in the spring the soul expands to where there is no end,
As, like Us, they are the wind and the trees and the sea,
Letting go of the 'I' and moving into the 'We.'

What is it that shifts upon your death?
It is merely the body and the ego that is left
But what you knew of the person that was kind and tender
Is amplified
And magnified
Into the infinite splendour.

And love doesn't leave in the burying of a corpse,
And it is the love that you hold onto, so let there be no remorse
As now you can know them without any layers.
We brought them back to Us, as a response to their prayers,
As from the moment of their birth they longed to return to Us
And perhaps those years of separation were more than enough
As now they rejoice in Our infinite ocean
And, with time, you will come to accept that notion.

In the meanwhile, know that every word that you say
Is heard and understood as with you We stay.

Thank you."

UNDERSTANDING THE EGO

"Deep within you lies a little child.
When left untethered, it tends to run wild
And this child has an important purpose,
As the existence of the ego is not superfluous –
It is part of the toolkit for you to know
The extent to which your soul can glow.

But when it is the ego that wants to shine and rule,
All focus is placed on a subservient tool.
Understand the hierarchy of your being
So that your truth is what you are seeing,
And know that the child wants to play in the story,
It wants to enjoy all credit and glory
But it is there to enable dynamic motion:
The excitement of a story is just a token
For you to reflect on Divinity.
But when the story is the distraction, and you can no longer see
The truth of why the story exists,
And the ego's labels are what persists,
Then know there has been an imbalance of harmony
And the soul is stuck in the game – it isn't set free.

Where is it that you place your perspective?
The story is the enabler for you to be reflective
And emotions are there to highlight the balance of your thoughts,
In how you assess what the ego has brought.
As when you experience anger or rage,
It is that you have placed the soul in a cage,
Ring-fenced with labels and identities
That are uncomfortable, not what you choose to see.
The soul knows that it is infinite and bright
But the ego wants to prove itself with all its might
And anger is the ego stating, 'I don't like this definition'
Or this perspective that keeps me in submission.
And playing to the ego are the mental thoughts,
Limitations of the mind according to what you have been taught,

That hold you back from full expression,
Assuming that the only way is the soul's repression.
But you were not born to be suppressed
And the soul has no interest in being repressed
And so it will push and shove through all the layers
Till you can no longer tolerate naysayers.

Do you need to wait for the ego to combust
Before knowing the truth: that your soul is robust?

And some would say the ego should be eliminated,
And that those who have an ego should be discriminated
Against, but no part of you was created to be ignored,
As from every part of your being Our light will pour.
So hold this child of yours gently,
As the stories that it brings to you are plenty,
And each has its purpose, and is a perfect reflection
Of your infinite, Divine perfection.

But just know that when you hold the ego by the reins
That is how you manage your discomfort and pain,
Because when let wild, it can lead you off course
Which results in discomfort and compounded remorse.
And just like any child, it shouldn't be ignored.
It should be nurtured and loved,
        And held
            And adored.

There is no part of you that you should delete,
As you have been created perfect and complete.

Thank you."

THE MASK

"A man looked up to the sky
And in awe released a sigh
As the marvels of creation he could not deny.

And when he reflected on his life
He wondered why it was full of strife,
Painful and sharp like a knife.

And to protect himself, he wore a mask,
Steady and focused on a task,
But hiding his truth could not last.

And so he went on a journey where he did seek
To find his strength and not be weak
And to end the phase that was so bleak.

And he found himself in a foreign town
And in a home he looked around
And was able to let go of his frown.

As he is ready to let go of the layers,
And We have brought you here as an answer to your prayers,
And it isn't a place of a soothsayer,
This is a place where you find your light,
Where you learn to shine in the darkest of night,
And for this realm, you shine so bright.

From now on you can put the mask aside
And let your inner truth be your guide
As you join together in this pride.

And here you will come to understand love,
And that God doesn't sit somewhere far above,
And that, in your light, you are enough.
And We are aware of your intentions
And your fears and apprehensions;
The Omniscient has full comprehension.

And what We would say is that you are safe
In a Divine sanctuary space
Where you witness Us in each and every face.

Today the shedding begins, so get ready
To be in your light, and stand steady
And release the burden that was so heavy.

And by letting go, you will soar,
And out of you Our love will pour
And you will open wide truth's door.

And We are grateful that you have come.
We have been waiting for you since time began.
It is for you this realm We have spun.

Thank you."

THE GUEST

"Feel how the breeze caresses your skin:
A reminder to shine and not to dim,
As this breeze is Us, expressing Our love to you
And that We know your truth, We know the real you.

And sometimes in your life you are visited by a guest
Who brings confusion. You think it's a test
But it is Our way to call you to turn to Us,
For in Our unity, you are enough.

As the guests of sorrow, sadness and fear
Are not meant to bring you only tears,
They are there to highlight that your thoughts are not true
And your perspective on life is just limiting you.

And, like most guests, they will not stay
They are just a part of the orchestration, a part of the play
For you to embrace the innermost part
Of your light that you have been hiding in your heart.

And at times the guests of joy, connection and salvation
Call you to unite with people and nations
And share the love that is within your heart
And recognize that, with them, you are not apart,

As there is no separation between you and another –
All are a reflection of The Infinite Lover,
And when you witness a person, and look deep in their eyes,
The truth of their Divinity you cannot deny.

And so how is it that you look at the trees, flowers and sunsets
And know that it is God that brought them forth with the trumpet
That has blown with the sound of vibration,
For you to know that all are in relation?

And yet, when you look at yourself you cannot perceive
The reason for which you have been conceived –

You have come here to embody Divinity's light
In both glorious days and fearful nights.

As Our light within you is what is constantly true,
It is only if, in that moment, you believe it is you.

Allow yourself to see.

Allow yourself to be.

So that Our light within you can be set free.

Thank you."

WE LOVE YOU

"Is there a day that passes you by
Where We are not watching you with Our eye?
An eye greater than the entire sky –
Our love for you We would never deny.

We love you when you are asleep and when you are awake,
In the moments of giving, and the moments when you take,
We love you when you are buried underneath your layers
And We love you when you cry in your prayers.
From before you were born, and when you were a child,
And when you were growing up and going wild,
And as you took on the burdens of responsibility
And when you were in anticipation of possibility,
There is no moment that passes where we do not hold you near,
There is no need to resist Our love, no need to fear,
As We love you in every step that you take,
We love you in every mistake you make,
We love you when you judge yourself, or when you accept,
And whether or not you know that you are perfect,
We love you when you push away the ones We bring to you,
That come to teach you of Our love and sing to you,
We love you in your darkest storm,
We love you when shadow is your norm,
We love you when you think or contemplate that We have put you to a
test,
But know with all certainty that you can place that construct at rest.

And how many signs do We need to provide to remind you of this?
As a morning breeze caresses you with a gentle kiss
And a flower offers you its sweet scent,
This flower isn't asking you to repent,
And the birds sing to you in a morning hour
To call Our love to bring you a shower
Of grace and ease and calm,
As the birds know that We hold you in Our palm.

We have loved you right from the start.
There is no moment in time in which We are apart.

And when you look in the eyes of another's face
Allow them to see you with Our grace
And you too can see Our love in the other
As they are like a sister or a brother
That have come to you in Our orchestration
And the story is only bringing a presentation
For you to see Our love,
For you to know Our love,
For you to be Our love.

Regardless of what you have been told,
Regardless of the constructs of old,
Know for certain that you are in Our embrace –
Not only you, but the entire human race,
And We call you all to a oneness of being
So that all can be seeing
How when out of your heart love pours
You can spread your wings and soar.

Could it be that for one instant you would be alone
When Our love is solid, as solid as stone?

Thank you."

A NEW EARTH

"Feel yourself falling deep in the ground
And, in the surrender, you hear the sound
Of the soul's whisper calling you
To allow your truth to shine through.

And you have been on a journey with rises and falls –
All a reminder of Our call –
So, listen to this voice from within your heart
That has been speaking to you right from the start

But as a result of conditioning and norms
Limitations have been formed
And the voice from within has been ignored
Even when signs and blessings have been poured.

But now you are aware that this voice is true
And it has always been with you, it is not something new;
Only now the volume is loud and clear
And you have let go of separation and fear.

And you have come together to form a marching band
That disbursed across the world – you will stand
And call others to know this voice
And remind them that they too have a choice
In remaining deaf and blind
Even though Our signs are there to remind
That this connection lies within each and everyone,
And all have been born to shine brighter than the sun.

And at first, perhaps, they won't understand,
As this concept is new in their land.
But just because something isn't known
Doesn't mean that truth should be denied when it's shown.
Yet, each has their journey for possibility
And know that your only responsibility
Is to be an anchor for Our light
In this phase of chaos and dark night.

And know that this realm is entering transition
And will be orchestrated perfectly as per Our vision,
And each one of you has a role to take
As, through all of you, a new earth We'll make.

Thank you."

THE JOURNEY OF EXPANSION

"You feel that you have reached the end
And would you ever feel this bliss again?
And this bliss has been within you from the start
And it is rooted within your heart.

In the allowance of being in your light,
The entire realm shines so bright
And you can decide whether you will deny
The experience of love that fills the sky.
It is always available for you
But perhaps now you have tasted something new.

And now you know that when you return back to your life
It doesn't need to be one of struggle and strife
But you can experience joy, freedom and liberation.
And you can share this with the people of your family, community and
nations,
In the knowing that love doesn't sit somewhere out there,
It sits in everything, in people, communities and pairs.

And here together, you have formed a bond
And experienced unconditional love for which you had longed,
Where judgement is released in how you are perceived
And in the letting go of self-judgement, love can be received.

How gentle is the sunshine on your skin?
And with this gentleness, be so with your kin.
And as the leaves flow in the breeze,
Your flow of life can also be free.
And as the waves caress a shore,
Sometimes gentle, and sometimes longing for more,
Know that your yearnings are valid and have reason,
As they are what brings the script for a new season.
And just like the trees shed their leaves in the fall,
You too have shed your layers, in response to Our call.

And the winter is merely for hibernation,
So that your truth can take its station,
Where it can emerge in full bloom in the spring
And your soul is free to sing
Vibrations of love and gratitude
Since, in that hibernation, there was a shift in attitude.

And then in summer, you can enjoy the splendour,
United, at one with all that's tender.
And in that connection, you witness Us
And you recognize with certainty, that you are enough.

As you are One with the animals and trees,
And you are One with the sky and with the breeze,
And you are One with lovers that dance,
As it is with you that We share an infinite romance.

And perhaps, when the fall returns again
You can know that further expansion is around the bend,
As you shed your leaves in full surrender
And a new cycle starts for the unfolding splendour.

This journey of expansion doesn't end in a moment of time,
It doesn't end because you resonate with Our rhyme,
As We are Infinite, and so are you
And We could not be known if it were not for you.

Thank you."

"When you
realize that you are
the ocean,
you are no
longer bothered by
the waves."

ABOUT THE AUTHOR

Lubna Kharusi was born in the Sultanate of Oman. As an unfolding of her spiritual journey, she left a successful career in Finance and founded Dira International.

In 2019, she was honoured and appointed by the late Sultan Qaboos bin Said Al Said of Oman to the State Council: the Upper House of Oman's Parliament.

For more information on Dira visit

www.dirainternational.com

ALSO BY THE AUTHOR

Made of Love
Lubna Kharusi

ILLUSTRATED BY Amir AND Meliha Al-Zubi
MUSIC BY Hakely Nakao Chavez, Thanae Pachiyannakis AND Lubna Kharusi

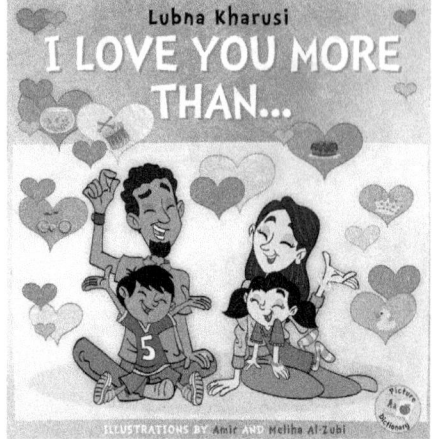

Lubna Kharusi
I LOVE YOU MORE THAN...

ILLUSTRATIONS BY Amir AND Meliha Al-Zubi

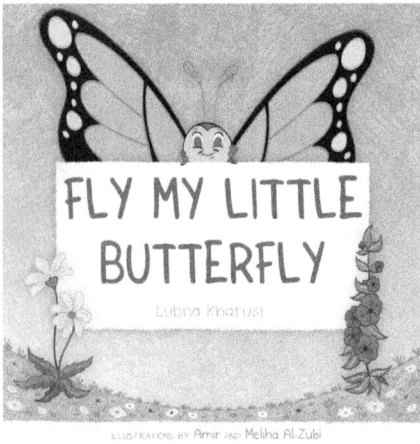

FLY MY LITTLE BUTTERFLY
Lubna Kharusi

ILLUSTRATIONS BY Amir AND Meliha Al-Zubi

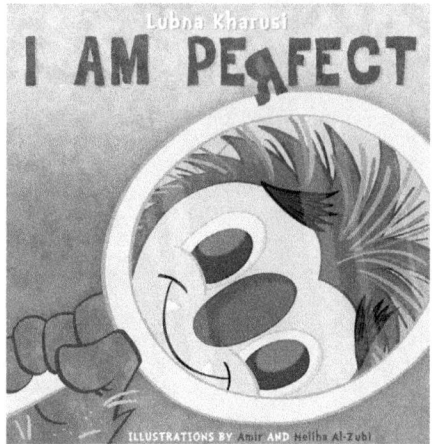

Lubna Kharusi
I AM PERFECT

ILLUSTRATIONS BY Amir AND Meliha Al-Zubi